MODERN FERRETING

MODERN FERRETING

David Brian Plummer

The Boydell Press · Ipswich

First published 1977 by The Boydell Press Ltd
PO Box 24, Ipswich IP1 1JJ

ISBN 0 85115 083 7

Photoset, printed and bound
in Great Britain by
Lowe & Brydone Printers Limited
Thetford, Norfolk

Contents

1 The Ancestor – The Polecat

Ferrets belong to a family called the mustelids – a large family comprising stoats, weasels, polecats, pine martens, badgers and wolverines. All are intensely predatory and have as a common denominator a courage which far exceeds their size. The very word stoat is probably derived from the Belgic word meaning bold or brave.

Ferrets were defined by early dictionary writers as partly domesticated or ill-tamed polecats, and here begins our problem. Which polecat was the ancestor of the domestic ferret? Europe possesses three types of polecat, the European, the Asiatic and the marbled polecat. A glance, however, at the marbled polecat which resembles a skunk, will convince even the most amateur of naturalists that it is not the ancestor of the modern ferret. Most early naturalists were of the opinion that the ferret was simply a domesticated Asiatic polecat. This animal still abounds in Asia and is found as far West as the plains of Bohemia. The creature closely resembles the ferret in shape and is sandy brown with darker coloured legs and tail. (There are many ferrets that are almost identical to the Asiatic polecat in colour.) This polecat lives largely on ground squirrels and supplements its diet with frogs, birds, snakes and probably insects. It is so easily tamed, that it is small wonder that the early naturalists believed it to be the ancestor of the ferret. Indeed, it may well have been the ancestor of some type of ferret, for it is said that Genghis Khan made use of these creatures in hunting. Little or no accurate research was done into the real ancestry of the ferret until the last fifty or so years. Now the modern naturalist began to take a new look at the humble ferret. From skull measurement, feeding and breeding habits it is now fairly certain that the Asiatic polecat was not the ancestor of the ferret. There are many who believe that Asiatic polecat blood did contribute to the origin of the ferret however. There is one school of geneticists who believe that man domesticates very wild animals simply by crossing two related species. This school of thought believes that man produced the very tame domesticated rabbit by crossing the rabbit with a hare. Thus the offspring of two slightly related but very wild creatures is thrown into what must only be called species confusion and is therefore extremely tame. These scientists believe man took the gentle Asiatic polecat and crossed it with the far more savage European species and *voilà* – the ferret was created. Sadly, interesting as this theory is, it does not bear up to close examination. I have tried to cross Asiatic polecats with ferrets and have had no success in spite of the fact that I used ferrets which exactly resembled the Asiatic polecat in colour. Perhaps I was unlucky in my attempts at hybridising but Lascelles, no mean naturalist by any standards, states that many of his keepers lost white albino ferrets last century and recovered them in kindle to wild British polecats. He states that the offspring were very dark, clever, strong and fierce and made excellent rabbiting ferrets. Furthermore the skull of a ferret reared on rats, rabbits, birds and other natural foods is identical to the skulls of European polecats. Haagerdoorn is not so convinced, however, for he states that the fitch, or European polecat, even if reared in captivity as it was in the pre-war Germany fur ranches, is totally intractable. Haagerdoorn suggested that several of these fur farms would have done well to have bred a more tractable strain by crossing the fitches with ferrets.

Haagerdoorn is, I believe, totally wrong. Stoats, weasels and polecats are all easily tamed if taken young. I have met numerous European naturalists who have captured wild polecat kittens and within a short time had them very tame – so tame that several were used as ferrets (Haagerdoorn states that to use a fitch for ferreting would be like taking a tiger out hunting). Some weeks before I started writing this book, I had a young stoat whose mother had been shot while carrying her kit to safety and had turned to fight off a golden labrador. It was about seven weeks old when it arrived and within two hours it would drink milk from the palm of my hand. I was all set for an attempt at hybridising my tame dog stoat with a jill ferret, when my Siamese cat put an end to my genetic dreams by killing my stoat.

As the reader will now have gathered, I believe that man simply took the kits of the European polecat, tamed them, and Eureka – the ferret came into existence. Let us now forget the Asiatic polecat and examine his European cousin – the real ancestor of the ferret.

The European polecat is practically identical with the polecat ferret or fitch, or fitchet ferret as they refer to it in the Midlands. The yellow undercoat has a thick covering of dark brown guard hairs. Like the fitchet ferret it has the typical "panda" type face. The average male is about $2\frac{1}{2}$-3 lb in weight, about the weight of a good useful line ferret, but the female is much smaller and may only be half the size of the male. It is said that in Cardiganshire a reddish species exists, identical in colouring to the sandy ferret. I'm afraid I am very suspicious of this polecat – it is a very suspect sub-species as far as I'm concerned, as I believe these to be descendants of feral ferrets – ferrets lost after a day's hunting. There are in fact many biologists who believe that there are no true polecats left in Britain and that all the specimens seen and recorded are simply feral ferrets. There is much evidence to suggest that the true wild British polecat became extinct during the nineteenth century.

Man had damned good reason to make this fierce little creature extinct. It was nearly impossible to keep poultry when this marauder moved into the district. The very word polecat is derived from the French *la poule* – a hen. The hen cat – a visit to the hen coop by this furious little predator – meant that morning would find the occupants dead with their craniums caved in. An escaped ferret will invariably forsake the rats and mice of the hedgerow for the poultry house and cause havoc as severe as that caused by a wild polecat. Once when I lived in Rotherham in a dingy terraced house, I kept a pair of ferrets in the back yard. One day the jill escaped and fortunately I heard of the damage caused by the ferret before actually being questioned about the loss. Like the real coward I was I raced to Doncaster market and bought a replica of my lost ferret and denied any knowledge of a marauding ferret. Keeping ferrets in a back yard made me unpopular enough, without my escaped ferrets making cadavers of all the local poultry which I knew would become prize birds, with breathtaking prices when I admitted to the ownership of the killer. For this reason no ferret owner will own up to the loss of a ferret until he is absolutely certain of the damage wrought.

Wild polecats have amazingly varied diets. They rarely stray far from water so amphibians and water fowl feature on their menus. I have in my possession the diary of one William Graham, a gamekeeper of maybe a hundred and ten years ago, written in the copperplate writing that was taught in the eighteenth century schools. Graham states that it was impossible for farmers to keep ducks when he came to the area on account of the raids by the polecats, for they attracted the polecats like magnets. He ends his paragraph with the cryptic comment: "I believe they come only for the ducks." Hubbard states that frogs are caught and bitten through the brain, but though paralysed, the leucotomised victims are still alive. They are then stored in holes for a rainy day when hunting is poor – a macabre living larder. Frogs will live with large areas of their brains cut away, so perhaps the ghoulish story has a ring of truth about it, though it does credit the polecat with an almost superhuman intelligence. Rabbits are eaten if they can be caught off guard underground, or bottled up in blind end galleries and slain by the brain bite, or have their hind quarters eaten off them, for both a polecat or a hungry ferret will, if it fails to make the fatal brain bite, eat the haunches off the live rabbit. Nasty, but God did not endow the polecat with those huge eye teeth in order for it to eat lettuce. Rats are reputedly taken by polecats although the male polecat is far too large to enter an average rat warren, and I believe that the female soon learns that a rat is just a little too much for her to handle and will look for less ferocious victims to satiate her blood lust, and blood lust it is – for all mustelids slay far more than they need. The almost insane frenzy of a ferret in a poultry house just has to be seen to be believed. One hen would satisfy the needs of a large hob ferret for a week – yet I know of no one who has had a ferret invade their poultry house, who did not see mass slaughter.

Many naturalists believe that fish are also taken by the wild polecat for he certainly swims well enough and is reputed to be able to dive. Few ferrets, however, enjoy swimming, though all enjoy splashing about in their water dishes. However, Andy Johnson, a close friend and a reliable witness, stated that his sandy hob swam out after a rat it had bolted from the Birmingham canal. Nearly all the ferrets I have used have had a marked aversion to water. Has man bred out this instinct or could it be that perhaps some Asiatic polecat blood (a creature which has aversion to water) is present in the blood of the domesticated ferret?

One feature which characterises the polecat is its obnoxious stench. Early European settlers in America referred to the skunk as a polecat. Beneath the tail of the polecat is found a small scent gland which produces a substance to mark its territory and just possibly to deter its enemies. When alarmed, the polecat empties the contents of this gland immediately and the stench is almost unbelievable. The odour lingers on clothes and hands and resists most attempts to remove it. This gave the polecat its Anglo-Saxon nickname the foul-

10

mart or foul marten to distinguish it from the pine marten or sweet marten, a creature closely resembling the polecat, but whose scent glands contain a musky, but not disagreeable, odour. The ferret retains this scent gland to an equal, or perhaps lesser extent, and when attacked or simply frightened badly, releases the gland fluid in a similar manner to the polecat. Some years ago I had a very hard, tough, terrier, which for no accountable reason developed a pathological hatred of my ferrets. He used to stand on his hind legs and lick the filth from the cage front near the dung corner and perhaps one nipped his tongue, maybe starting the feud. Feud it was however, for at that time I had a score or more adult ferrets. One day when I was digging my forlorn looking garden he left me and decided to slay the whole batch of ferrets, but the stench remained on his fur for a fortnight in spite of frequent baths.

Another quality possessed by the polecat and sadly capitalised on by man, is its utter fearlessness – a characteristic of all stoats and kindred. When faced with danger, polecats are more likely to fight than run. Thorburn in his magnificent book *Mammals* (a treasure, if only for its glorious colour prints) states that one day his brother found a polecat eating a rat. He went closer to the beast to investigate it and the polecat flew at him in blind rage to protect its kill. There is an epitaph-type poem to a northern terrier (breed unimportant and undefined) which was noted for its courage. It would face a foulmart or draw a brock, proof indeed of the fighting qualities of the polecat. John Tucker Edwardes, creator of the Sealyham, then one of the gamest breeds alive, knew all about the ferocity of the polecat. Edwardes tested the courage of his dogs in a gory, merciless, way. He would encourage one of the keepers in his estate called Sealyham (hence the name of the terrier) to trap wild adult live male polecats. The polecat would be rolled inside the trap until it was in a state of chattering fury. Edwardes would then bring along a team of yearling puppies (and Sealyhams really are puppylike at a year old). He would open the cage and urge the puppy to rush in, and draw out the maddened polecat. Those who refused were put down instantly and the game terriers were added to his badger hunting pack. As a breeder of terriers I shudder at this hellish test for a yearling puppy.

During the eighteenth and nineteenth centuries the Lakelands and Wales held several bobbery packs composed of hounds, long dogs and terriers in order to hunt polecats – for not only did the animal rank as a grade A pest to all poultry keepers, but it provided excellent sport by dint of its fighting ability. This alone would be proof of the valour of a beast only two and a half times the size of an adult rat.

As I have stated there was a time when it was profitable to breed polecats or fitches in captivity. The fur, termed as fitch, is very beautiful but unless they are killed by instant electrocution or by carbon monoxide poisoning (as are mink) then the sense of approaching death causes the scent glands to explode and the pelt is permanently ruined by the lingering smell. At one time I kept the pelts of eight polecat hob ferrets, dried them and had them cured, but they still had a nasty musky smell. This, of course, could be explained by the fact that they had been killed by the vendetta-minded terrier mentioned previously. After four years the smell still lingered, so I threw them away, for they were so aromatic no furrier wanted to buy them – though a few expressed interest in their quality. Fashions changed and fitch pelts became rare as breeders went over to farming his more valuable cousin – the mink. Recently one of the fur breeding magazines mentioned a new interest in fitch production in the south of England. The pelt of the polecat or polecat ferret is remarkably beautiful. I once showed a huge hob liner to a friend of mine's wife who was employed by the Royal Shakespeare Theatre company. This beautiful hob was my pride and joy, but I put him back in his cage when I saw by the look on her face that she saw him as a fur collar, not as a rabbit hunter.

Wild polecats avoid thickly wooded areas, preferring open fields and hedgerows to the forests. Reports that they are often seen in the vicinity of towns and villages should be viewed with a little suspicion. More than likely these are simply feral ferrets. Both polecats and wild ferrets will utilise any form of shelter, be it a deserted burrow, rat warren, cairn of stones or wood pile. One of my escaped pregnant jills once reared a litter of six young in a wood pile half a mile from my house. How they lived I do not know, as myxomatosis had already wiped out the area's rabbit population and the jill had long ago realised rats were too much for her, but her litter were in excellent health and she was as fat as butter.

The female polecat breeds once a year. After a period of gestation lasting roughly six to seven weeks, a litter of three to eight young are born, totally naked. By about three to four weeks old they will voraciously suck meat from a kill brought to the nest by the dam, but

12

in spite of the fact that they will hiss, spit and even fruitlessly attack the hand of an intruder, they are still totally blind until they are thirty to thirty-six days old. Rats, rabbits and rodents of all kinds are able to see well at fourteen days old, but all mustelids are totally blind for a considerable period of time. There is a purpose in this lengthy period of blindness for it ensures that the young remain nest bound until they are able to take care of themselves. In fact the young are not totally independent until they are five months old.

Curiosity, which is a feature of all mustelids, is frequently their undoing. No mustelid can forgo investigating any new object. Tunnels and holes just have to be explored, every nook and cranny investigated, for like all intelligent animals (and predatory animals always have a higher intelligence than their herbivorous victims) the ferret and polecat are inquisitive. A ferret allowed into a house investigates every gap under every piece of furniture, every fold of a carpet and every corner of a room. Subsequently all mustelids, polecats in particular, find any tunnel trap nothing short of irresistible and consequently the foulmarten, never welcome on any game estate, passed into near or total extinction. They just had to go. The nineteenth century was the age of the professional keeper and keepers had little trouble ridding the estate of these psychopathic little killers. William Graham states that he managed to trap twelve in one night all within the confines of his Hampshire estate.

The polecat is nocturnal and rarely ventures out at day time. If he is forced to leave his lair during daytime he attracts considerable attention from birds – particularly the crow family. Few crows, magpies and jays can resist mobbing a polecat abroad by day. This is a useful fact when one is trying to find an escaped ferret. I have found many ferrets (quite a few not my own, I confess) simply by watching the mobbing action of crows. The dark polecat ferret attracts considerable interest from the crows, jays and magpies. This peculiar reaction can be put to good use by keepers who wish to rid a shoot of magpies (who just cannot leave an escaped ferret alone). A dark hob ferret tied on a line in the middle of a field within shooting distance of a well made hide, is nothing short of a death trap to magpies. They just cannot resist mobbing him. Even when they see their numbers shot they stick around fascinated by the sight of the ferret ambling around on his line. A friend of mine actually stepped out of the hide and slew a magpie with a male goshawk I once owned, but in spite of the sight of one of their number being

13

slain by the hawk, the magpies still returned to mob the ferret. Crows, magpies and kin folk are curious birds and curiosity not only kills cats, but obviously crows, rooks and polecats.

The fact that the polecat is a creature of the night, made him a subject to be used in spells, potions and suchlike. One grimoire (a book of spells) suggests that a remedy for cleaning gangrenous, septic or dead flesh from a wound was to kill a polecat, and smooth the freshly skinned pelt on to the necrotic or dead tissue. The pelt is suddenly, and with great force, ripped off. The dead flesh sticks to the pelt (which is then thrown into a fire and burned) and the wound is cleaned. At first I thought this simply a case of "magic by association" that is the polecat savagely attacks its prey, therefore, the pelt might be expected to savagely attack the septic flesh. I had dismissed the idea, until I met a Finnish doctor who stated that Lapps, smitten with frost bite, use the still warm, wet skins of lemmings (hardly predatory) for similar purposes. Furthermore, she assured me she had seen the result of this treatment and in a rough crude bush surgery way, it had worked.

Another legend which concerns both the Asiatic polecat and its European relative is that they are credited with the gifts of being almost supernatural thieves. Just as Brer rabbit is the noted rogue and "wide boy" of Negro American folk legend, the polecat occupies the same position in the European myth. They are reported to be extremely cunning at the theft of eggs, milk and suchlike. I doubt whether these legends would bear up to an investigation but it does perhaps explain the word for the domesticated polecat – for the word ferret is dervied from the Latin *fur* – a thief. So we leave the polecat and pass on to his domesticated cousin, the ferret.

2 The Ferret

"Forget it, you'll find nothing but a maze ending in blind alleys." This was the advice given to me by one of the foremost authorities on the history of domestication of animals, when I visited his home in the countryside around West Berlin. I had by now convinced myself that the ferret was simply a descendant of the European polecat and was now out to find out when or possibly where this domestication had taken place – literally to place a "circa" something or another around the time when polecats became ferrets. "You'll find some references, but little that will bear up to any proper investigation." "Good luck though," he added, "I hope you have more luck than I had." On this daunting note I left this gracious gentleman and began a search which was to make Jason's search for the Golden Fleece seem like a treasure hunt staged by the Young Conservative Club.

When first researching any animal, be it horse, sheep or cow, the seeker after truth would do well to go back to one of man's earliest reference books – the Bible, and lo and behold, I scored my first direct hit in Leviticus II, Verse 30, of the James Edition – or so I thought. There was the reference to the ferret as being an animal the Jews were forbidden to eat – I doubt whether the ferret would have proved a very tempting delicacy even to one of the famished horde of Moses, but even if one was found, it was not to be regarded as food. It was all so easy – too easy in fact, Leviticus written some time after Moses and some time before David. Easy to date, but I had now very severe doubts. Why had my Berlin professor not discovered this (he spoke fluent Hebrew and was far better versed with the Old Testament than I was ever likely to be). He had not even directed my course of investigation towards the Bible. Something was very wrong. I went to an early Hebrew version of Leviticus, began translation and came back bitterly disappointed. The animal referred to in Leviticus II, Verse 30, was certainly not my ferret. I wrote to an authority on the dietary laws of the Jews in

Tel Aviv. He wrote back confessing that he was also very unhappy about the creature referred to as being translated as "a ferret". I notice in the Revised Edition of the Bible that the translation had been changed to "land lizard", whatever that may be, but one thing was certain, I was back at square one.

I had a stroke of luck some eight months later. I was reading a copy of Strabo's book *Geographica* in a local bookshop (I read a chapter a day, which prevented my having to buy the book) when the word ferret leapt at me. He stated that the Romans kept these ferrets to run around their villas to keep down rats and mice. I hastily, though with a sad heart, bought the book. I had at last reached my goal. Strabo wrote around the second century after Christ. He was erudite and accurate so I could place my dating of the domestication as somewhere prior to AD 200. Once again I had my sneaking doubts, and they also proved well founded. I obtained a copy of Strabo's work in Latin and set to work. Yes, it was ferret allright, but it was prefixed by Lybian and my heart sank. No true polecat existed in Africa – though perhaps Strabo had merely stated that the variety of ferret was referred to as the Lybian, just as we talk about the 'Belgian hare' domestic rabbit, which is neither a Belgian nor a hare. Something amiss here. No, I was convinced that the animal referred to by Strabo was not the ferret, but almost certainly the Egyptian mongoose – not as smelly as the ferret and though not as fond of snakes as his Indian cousin in Kipling's *Rikki Tikki Tavi,* he was reputed to be mustard on rats. I found proof of this in a quaint archaic booklet entitled *Mice and Rats as the Enemies of Man.* There had been an invasion of brown rats in the West Indies and someone had offered a prize for anyone who could offer a solution to curbing the rats. The Egyptian mongoose had been introduced (a very close relative of the ferret) and in the short time had reduced the number of rats, but alas, like the ferret, he is a confirmed chicken killer and soon became such a pest to poultry keepers that dogs were imported to hunt him down. Strabo's beast was not my ferret. Welcome back Square One.

There is a quaint old Jewish saying that states: "Before one decides on the cure for a serpent bite, first decide on the serpent that has bitten you." This line of research was to be just a little more rewarding. I had first to find why man had domesticated the fierce, smelly, polecat. Clearly not as a pet, for though I find ferrets endearing, the smell would have prevented the ordinary man wanting

Polecat or fitch hob and jill – note small size of jill compared with larger, stronger and less versatile hob.

one as a pet. Ferrets or domesticated polecats had to have come into creation as animals to assist the hunter, but to hunt what? Certainly not brown rats, for they reached Europe around 1700 and I had a woodcut of a warrener using ferrets dated around 1100. It was certainly not domesticated to curb the black rat which reached Europe on board returning crusading ships sometime after AD 984. These were most unsuitable animals to hunt with ferrets. Few ferrets were small enough to get down the holes, as the rats were very small, and when they bolted, being as they were originally tree dwellers, they simply scampered up to the roof with the grace of a squirrel – far beyond the reach of the ferret. The polecat was tamed quite simply to hunt the humble rabbit.

Now the rabbit, a pest in most parts of the world, originally occupied only a small strip of country – namely the extreme South of Spain, the Balearic Islands and perhaps North Africa. It had spread to the rest of Europe, and indeed the rest of the world, through the agencies of man, who had captured it, tamed it, and then released it in different countries. Now I was fairly certain that the rabbit came to Britain through the agencies of the Romans or the Phoenicians, both of whom overran the rabbit's native lands and did in turn visit Britain. The Phoenicians came for trade in tin and the Romans came for conquest. Now Semitic people such as Jews,

17

Sandy or diluted polecat hob.

Arabs and Phoenicians are loath to touch creatures like rabbits, so to my mind it had to be the highly omnivorous Romans who found even dormice fried in honey edible (hence the edible dormouse). Thus the European peoples had the answer to the rabbit problem by simply domesticating the wild, but easily tameable European polecat. Therefore, I would place the dating of the domestication of the ferret as sometime after Christ, but as a way out should I be proven wrong – in Spain and the rabbit's native lands perhaps earlier. Zeuner believes the ferret came to Britain with the Normans as he can find no reference to the ferret in Anglo Saxon literature, but there is a great scarcity of Anglo Saxon literature and a great shortage of any literature on the ferret at any time, so perhaps Zeuner's work might not bear up to close examination. I was reminded of my mentor's words: "You'll find some references to ferrets, but few that will bear up to examination." I should have listened to him. I had become a joke in the university libraries of Britain and had been christened by my close friends the "ferret king" – I certainly had little concrete evidence to show for my two years of research.

Early ferrets were almost certainly fitch or polecat coloured – the other forms appearing as mutations or sports in polecat-coloured litters and kept and propagated by way of being a novelty. Basically three colour varieties exist in the ferret: the fitch or polecat ferret,

18

an animal almost identical to the wild European polecat; a sandy or pale brown, diluted form of the above; and the albino form which can vary from very pure white to almost dirty yellow. I am frequently asked which colour ferret makes the best hunter and I am forced to reply "Colour does not count." Considering polecats, sandies and whites can and do appear in the same litter it should be obvious that Ike Matthews' comments in his book on rat catching are bunkum. Matthews states that sandies, popular in the Midlands, were of little use for the task of ratting as they were usually lazy and cowardly. I am literally amazed that Matthews can state this. Firstly, if these ferrets had all these faults, then why were they popular in the Midlands? My own observations do not confirm those of Matthews, for I have seen good and bad sandy ferrets. Sometime in 1974 I lost a great number of jills through bad maulings from rats that lived on a particularly filthy tip in Yorkshire. On my way back from hunting I stopped the van at a filthy poultry yard run by two eccentric brothers, both batchelors, and both filthy dirty. They rarely worked and lived on rabbits they had poached and on clearing rats from local farmers. Their general appearance would have put off a tinker from purchasing goods from them, but they had the best litter of sandy ferrets I have ever seen. The ferrets were fed rats, rabbit entrails and crippled fowl and as a result of the diet were in first class fettle. I negotiated price with them, went through all the motions of walking away when they asked an astronomical figure (for they considered anyone who spoke anything that faintly resembled grammatical English as suckers) and finally bought the litter. The whole litter were excellent – they were excellent on rabbits and the jills were tigers to rats. I still keep this family though the bloodline is now diluted and I still have a large number of sandy ferrets appearing in my litters.

Many people favour white ferrets rather than sandies or fitch polecats. The reason for this is fairly obvious. A white ferret is easily seen when emerging from an earth, particularly if the hole is in heavy cover. Ray Hemming, a noted Midland ferreter, states that this is a load of bunkum. Ray believes that if one has ferreted efficiently and quietly then there is such an atmosphere of tension that one is able to hear a leaf fall, let alone a ferret creep from an earth. Furthermore, ferrets are usually very noisy in heavy cover and a ferret emerging from an earth in deep undergrowth, makes far more din than a fox bolting in similar circumstances. Still it is usually fairly

White hob.

easy to lose a ferret in a large warren, particularly in early Autumn when cover is still thick, so perhaps there may be something in the theory that a white ferret is less easily lost, as its colour does stand out against the English countryside.

There is yet another school that will not touch a white ferret with a barge-pole. All sorts of reasons are given for their dislikes and many of the reasons contain a grain of truth. The white ferret is an albino and the side effects of albinism are held in some suspicion by many countrymen. In fact any white animal be it albino or merely white, is often viewed with the same caution. Many hunters, particularly those in the north, will avoid using white terriers as they regard white colouration as being a hallmark of weak constitution. White puppies which appeared in Cairn litters were destroyed at birth as they were thought to be weaker than their darker brethren. (Eventually the West Highland White Terrier appeared as a result of breeding from these white Cairns.) Frankly little is known about the side effects of albinism. Human albinos frequently have sight defects and blister badly in bright sunlight. This is, however, hardly a problem in ferrets who do not rely on sight but hunt by scent and sound. In fact the darker forms of ferret all seem remarkably short sighted. The fur protects the skin from blistering even in the brightest sunlight, so albinism is therefore no problem in these respects.

There is now the matter of constitutional weakness to dispose of.

20

Many ferreters believe that white ferrets are more prone to mange than the darker varieties and are the first to die of "sweats". This same school believes that white ferrets tire more quickly after a hard day's work. Firstly, let us look at the legend of white ferrets contracting mange more quickly. Here, as in most legends, there is perhaps a basis in truth. Follicular mange – a type of dog mange, is rarely contracted by humans, but sometimes people with very fair skins do contract this disorder. Ferret mange is sarcoptic mange however. A totally different mite which infects black or white animals and people equally. Thus, a ferret that is an albino can look dreadful with a bad attack of mange as the skin is naturally pink and looks very bad when inflamed. At one time I fed unskinned foxes to my ferrets, for we were killing a large number of foxes at that time. We were frequently troubled with mange, as foxes are riddled with sarcoptic mange mites (a slightly different variety from the species which infects dogs). All colours became infected though I confess the white ferrets looked worse because of their pink skin. Incidentally, human beings can and do pick up mange mites from ferrets; the condition is then known as scabies.

"Sweats" or ferret distemper, is identical to canine distemper and ravages all three colours with equal savagery. A few years ago I had an infected bitch brought to my kennels to mate. All my ferrets died and I noticed that all three colour phases went down to this dreaded malady. Next let us debunk the weakness-of-the-constitution old wives' tale. Most strains of commercial rabbits (bred for meat) are albino, they are almost permanently in kindle, and are very vigorous and healthy in spite of their lack of pigmentation. Frankly it makes not a whit of difference what colour your ferret is, providing it is healthy, well nourished and active. It is purely a matter of taste. I like sandy ferrets because my first really good ferret was a sandy, but all my close ferreting associates confess to the same reasons for their likes and dislikes of the three colour phases.

Size, however, is important. Hobs, which are male ferrets, are usually much bigger than the jills so subsequently they are not as versatile as the smaller jill ferrets. Hobs are usually far too big to enter a rat warren – a task which even a large jill has little difficulty in negotiating. I have little use for large hobs except as line ferrets (I will explain later the task of the line ferret). They are useless for rat as they cannot get down even a large rat burrow and I do not like them for working to rabbit, for a large hob is so heavy

Polecat hob.

that once they grip a rabbit underground the rabbit cannot bolt even if it wishes to, and is killed down the hole before it has a chance to make the surface.

For general work, I find a medium sized jill hard to beat. They find little problem getting into a rat hole and are sufficiently large to give a good account of themselves against a rat. They are useful for rabbiting, not too light to get knocked about by the rough and tumble dealt out by a rabbit below ground, but still sufficiently small to allow a rabbit to bolt should it wish to do so. Furthermore, I find that a medium sized jill has less trouble in producing her kits than very tiny females who often experience parturition problems. Very tiny jills do have their uses however – some of my best friends swear by them. Tiny jills do, however, often get badly knocked about by rats, for a good sized rat can reach nearly a pound in weight. I once had a tiny dark polecat jill that I bought from a vermin controller in Sheffield. I feel he must have used Warfarin more than ferrets, for his stock was rarely handled. When I first picked up this jill she bit me savagely and hung on. I immediately christened her Medusa after the singularly unpleasant lady Gorgon. I also bought her larger sister, much bigger but equally vicious. Medusa was utterly fearless with rat, but lacked the size to cope with a large buck or doe rat that was prepared to slug it out. Medusa became fearfully knocked about but always went back for more. One day, after a particularly lengthy duel with a large rat which she had bolted and had been nabbed by my terriers, Medusa emerged from the earth very bloody and shaking herself. She had one eye bitten out of the socket and had a fearful slash on the throat. She was still keen to go back and try for another, but I retired her from rat hunting from then on. She became an excellent rabbit hunter, however. Her sister, twice her size, became a very useful ratter and rarely suffered from the severe maulings that Medusa had sustained. A ratting ferret should be nearly as big as an adult buck rat to last long in the sport of ratting. I believe using any ferret smaller than this to be very hard on the ferret.

3 Choosing A Ferret

Having by now decided exactly what you want by way of colour and sex, the time has now come to choose your ferret. Now for the first piece of concrete advice of the book – let your first ferret be a youngster. You will be able to mould this ferret yourself – mould it well, gentle it and train it, and it will serve you well. You will have moulded the ferret and if it finishes up a ruined skulking brute which lies up at every chance, then you, and only you, will be to blame. Purchase an older trained ferret, however, and you may well achieve some success. You may, however, inherit all the problems of mis-training and mishandling instilled in it by its previous owner. The would be purchaser might wish to hunt rat. If so he would be well advised to realise that after a period of time your jill will begin to realise that the rat is a little too much for her and she will refuse to enter the rat warren. If the buyer purchases a young ferret then he will probably achieve a longer period of rat hunting before his jill quits. The buyer may also find that the older animal he has purchased has long ago realised the fury of the rat and will refuse to enter to them. She may scream, wriggle, bite and do anything rather than go in and face the rat.

OK, so rat hunting is not for you and you really want a ferret for rabbiting. Again take my advice – choose a young ferret and avoid an old trained ferret like the plague. I am always sceptical about buying a grown terrier, a grown lurcher, or an adult ferret. People who sell adult animals invariably have a damned good reason for wanting to get rid of them. The terrier will be either too hard or refuses to stay underground, the lurcher will either give tongue (fatal to poachers) or have "blown" (a damaged heart or diaphragm) and the man who wants to sell an adult ferret is always suspect. A good rabbiting ferret is literally worth its weight in gold and no one will want to sell such a treasure. A close friend of mine was offered an incredible sum for an excellent jill that not only never lay up, but dragged out young rabbits whenever she could. Jeff refused the money saying that he could make that sort of money in a week with such a jill. When an adult is offered for sale there is usually something amiss, for it has usually developed some fault which makes it undesirable. It may have developed the habit of latching on to the rabbit, killing it and sleeping on the warm carcase – a hard act to follow and a harder habit to break. Another annoying habit it may have is skulking – that is remaining near the mouth of the earth and refusing to come out. If you put in your hand, it moves back into the earth, just out of reach. Such a ferret can spend a whole afternoon just staring out with a look of paranoia. It is a habit brought about by mishandling when young – the young ferret bolted a rabbit, followed it up, was snatched up for its troubles and it left a bad impression on the animal. A person who does this will usually repeat the performance snatching up the ferret and reinforcing the dislike of the human hand. The ferret now permanently stays out of reach of the offending hand. Skulking is maddening – I have seen hunters driven to despair by it and shoot the ferret. Others merely get the ferret out by devious means and sell it – to you. It is nearly impossible to break skulking, so beware. It's dollars to doughnuts your vendor's ferret will have one of the above faults or why is he selling it? There are also other strange habits that will cause the owner to part with his ferret. A friend of mine once bought a ferret from a travelling man – people I call tinkers and town dwellers call itinerants. The tinker sold the hob for a very low price and I wondered what horror was to await us when we took him out. We took the hob out in October and I waited for the worst. For an hour I had a sudden feeling that John had "put one over" on the tinker. It was a real treasure, one of the gentlest hobs I have ever seen, fast, agile and one of the best bolters I have ever seen. Rabbit after rabbit hit the nets with the hob coming to the mouth to investigate and then straight back to work. This was indeed the bargain of bargains, gentle to handle and superb at his job – but now the tale takes a turn for the worse. No more rabbits were bolting and we were about to take up the nets. The hob emerged sniffing the mouth of the earth. However, he was now a changed creature, tail fluffed out and spitting like a hell cat. A lamb had entered the earth and a tiger had emerged. Some ferrets get very excited when hunting so I let him calm down. After a few minutes John bent to pick him up. He struck with the speed of a cobra at John's hand and latched on. It was a death-like grip which tightened as we pinched his paws and tail. He hung on like a bulldog, giving John's hand a savage shake. We began to walk to the nearby brook half a mile away with the ferret still hanging on like grim death, giving the hand a shake to remind John he was still alive. Ferret teeth are like hypodermic needles and do not cause the pain that a rat bite causes, but the tightening of the grip on the bone of a knuckle, followed by a violent shake as the ferret tries to dislodge a piece of flesh is agonising. I suggested that John lowered him into the stream so that by dint of shutting off his air supply, he would release his grip. It was a last resort, all other methods had failed. John immersed the hob until the head was below the level of the water. Fear made the beast tighten its grip still more. John now writhed in pain, but after two or three minutes, which to John seemed like several months, the ferret now unconscious floated to the top. Now I do not believe that qualities such as malice, cowardice and brutality exist in animals, for they are properties found only among men. I was, therefore, prepared to try to find a reason for this odd behaviour. A fox lodged at the rear of the earth, or maybe a badger approaching puberty driven from his native sette and settled in the warrren could have caused this fear reaction in the ferret, and I was prepared to give it a try. John, with his shirt soaked in blood, seemed oddly less enthusiastic. Next week we tried again – a shallow sette with two holes. One ferret in – one rabbit out, followed alas by the Jekyll now turned Hyde ferret, who repeated his performance on John's hand. John had boasted so much about how he had put one over on the traveller that as we were again half drowning off a ferret, Mark Wibley, our local wit, said, like a man quoting Keats, "Somewhere in far off Tewkesbury a tinker is laughing." John boxed up the ferret and sold it (for a profit) at Penkridge market. We looked for weeks to see a man with a crippled hand in Cannock, but we never found one. The ferret was undoubtedly schizophrenic – crazy as a coot when he came out of an earth, hard to manage when hunting, yet gentle as a lamb at home. What strange error of mishandling had caused this peculiar reaction or was it simply a slightly mad ferret? Moral of story – buy only a young ferret.

Right, we are all set to purchase a young ferret, but where do we go to obtain one. To those who are new to ferreting, and whose knowledge of purchase is through far off advertisements in *Exchange and Mart* it must seen quite a task to obtain a good young ferret. Let us now analyse the potential ferret sources.

The most obvious place to buy a ferret may, at first sight, be a gamekeeper and the would be purchaser might be fairly certain that if he went to a keeper at the end of August most keepers would have young ferrets for sale. Let me now debunk another legend. Keepers are vastly over-rated hunters and many of their sage-like pieces of advice passed on to a tyro ferret keeper belong in a joke book rather than a manual of ferreting. Furthermore, today keepers are reasonably well paid and find it easier to Cymag the earths rather than supplement their income from selling ferreted rabbits. Hence their ferrets are rarely used and not often handled – the result is often an extremely savage young ferret being purchased. Drabble, in his *Pedigree Unknown,* states that he had a hellish experience with a keeper-bought ferret that bit through flesh and bone. He was overcharged, sold a savage beast which had to be returned, and I could find the reader a hundred people who could tell him similar stories. Keepers invariably price their ferrets too highly as they do their terriers, for people who don't really understand country ways and hunting must regard "keeper bred ferrets or terriers as a sure indication of quality". Keepers usually have ferrets for sale and if they are tame and reasonably priced then buy one, but don't for one minute imagine that the fact that your ferret was bred by a keeper places it a cut above other ferrets.

Backyard breeders are a good bet if one goes at the end of August when the young ferrets are eating him out of house and home. Again consider buying only if the price is right. Again remember every backyard breeder's stuff is bred from the best jill in England (for owning up to having a bad jill is tantamount to admitting that one is a bad driver or has an unfaithful wife). Men who are habitual poachers (or ardent rat hunters) and make their money from the sales of illicitly taken rabbits are usually fairly safe bets. They will have little use for skulkers and ferrets which habitually lie up, and their failures will have been sold long ago or put in a bucket of water – for nothing makes a man look and feel more naked than frantically digging to get out a ferret that has lain up when a policeman or gamekeeper ambles across the field towards him totally aware that the poacher is not going anywhere without his ferret. Furthermore, as an added advantage, many of these country poachers have large families who insist on the children cleaning out the ferrets while Dad sleeps off the effects of a hard night's lamping. Children cannot resist playing with baby ferrets and hence the young are usually as tame as kittens. One more sign to watch before purchase, however. Many poachers have strange ideas of the dietary needs of a ferret and tend to feed bread and milk slop as a staple diet. This produces chronically weak young ferrets that are frankly not worth purchasing. Watch the ferrets being fed; if they are slop fed, think twice about purchase. True you may be able to pick up a good young ferret or two but the chances are that you will buy a beast riddled with rickets as a result of malnutrition induced by the owner's stupidity. I confess I've lost a few sales when people come to buy a young ferret from me and find my youngsters tearing apart a freshly killed rat. A rat, however, is crammed full of the vitamins that bread and milk sop is lacking. Rat is a natural food and a ferret's gut is equipped only to deal with flesh, a bread and milk diet is foreign to the gut of a carnivore, so subsequently the pale white diarrhoea of the slop fed ferrets dung corner is the consequence. Another problem I have mentioned is rickets which usually manifests itself in deformities of the back legs which seem too weak to take the weight of the body – the back legs are splayed out behind the ferret so that the animal slithers around like a miniature seal. I saw two litters of these for sale in Bromsgrove – don't touch them with a barge pole – they are deformed through lack of calcium coupled with lack of vitamin A and D. The problem shouldn't concern you – don't buy them. John Davenham is doing some research into this condition in ferrets and allied species. He believes that such conditions could be hereditary and/or could be due to lack of sunlight. In human skin sunlight can help synthesise vitamins to counteract this deficiency. In ferrets I doubt if they can, for polecats are nocturnal and probably lack the necessary skin chemicals which can utilise the sunlight. He may be right about heredity however. I have seen some damnable deformities result through inbreeding ferrets and a tendency to rickets may be one of the hereditary factors. Frankly I attribute it all to diet. A ferret fed properly on flesh, bone and blood, just does not have these deformities. The reasons, once again, should not concern you – do not buy a deformed ferret. Stay clear of dietary and genetic freaks and purchase only a healthy, lively, animal. Once, in Doncaster market, I saw a litter of slightly underfed polecat ferrets with huge carnassial teeth which prevented the ferret from closing its mouth properly. John Latimer, a biologist friend of mine, states that he has seen quite a few litters of these deformed creatures – to my mind brought about by indiscriminate inbreeding, but perhaps even by dietary deficiency or disease. I have, in the nest at the time of writing, a litter of healthy ferrets with very short, kinky, tails. Not a serious deformity – though a result of in-breeding, but a prelude of bad things to come unless I outcross my ferrets with new blood. There is a move afoot to breed self docking Jack Russell terriers. It is a move that I oppose as any truncation of vertebrae is surely an indication that the genetic make up of the creature is slightly awry. As soon as I spot a deformity I bring in new blood and stop inbreeding, thereby avoiding sickening recessives appearing in future litters. Jills often eat litters when any malformities appear in them.

Avoid purchasing a sluggish ferret. Young stock should race up the bars as soon as a new visitor arrives. Even if it is not feeding time they should, if they are healthy, be curious to see new people. A litter that is slow to do this is best avoided. Maybe a coli bug has infected them (deadly), perhaps feline infectious enteritis (they'll be dead by the time you get home), or even the famous "sweats" is the cause of the lack-lustre. Don't buy or touch one. All these diseases will be passed on to the next poor devil you visit who will not thank you for introducing these infections.

So, at last, you find a litter bounding with health, eagerly racing around the cage like "Wall of Death riders", investigating all the comings and goings of your arrival. Stage one accomplished – they are fit. Examine the dung corner, faeces should be firm and black – then maybe these are the ferrets for you. Maybe – for there are other maladies to watch out for. If the ferrets have thin fur and inflamed patches, this is mange which not only infects your ferret, but will cause you considerable embarrassment when your child is excluded from school with scabies – for ferret mange is quite simply scabies. Early ferreting books state that mange is brought about by dirty cages – true, it doesn't help, but mange has to be introduced from somewhere, usually through hunting a fox earth or rat warren. Once the ferret is infected, filthy pens help to propagate this irritating mite. Clean cages do not mean absolute freedom from mange, but they help check this problem.

A far nastier, and more difficult to cure, malady is the almost legendary foot rot. Ferrets infected with this tread very carefully putting their feet down gingerly. They have damned good cause to, for much of the sole of the foot has been eaten away by the ravages of the fungus which causes this problem. This disease thrives in filth and wet floors. Early mink keepers found that mink also suffered from this when kept in wooden floored cages. Mink are kept on wire floors now which are dry and easily cleaned for the faeces and urine run through the floors. I do not like these cages for ferrets, for they are cold and inhospitable, but these cages certainly discourage foot rot. We use dry deal shavings, cleaned daily, and never get this problem. Anyway foot rot should not concern the buyer – the first sign of it should be enough to make him reach for his hat and coat and say "Goodbye – no thanks". Mange is fairly easy to cure, as it is caused by a tiny mite. Foot rot is caused by a fungus and is frankly hell to cure. Do not buy a ferret with any of these maladies – there will be plenty more healthy ferrets to buy during August. Don't even consider buying a doubtful ferret.

As I have stated, the time to buy ferrets is late August – as soon as they are able to feed well and run about. The reasons are fairly obvious. Firstly, the ferrets are not old enough to learn bad habits. Secondly, the ferrets at this age can easily eat a man out of house and home. A jill ferret with a litter of ten, healthy, ten week old young, will eat the same quantity of food as an adult alsatian and provide the owner with a constant source of worry about where to procure food for them. A ferret keeper who feeds birds, rats and rabbits, will find himself hunting full time to sustain the ravenous brood. At the time of writing I placed a big, stillborn pig weighing four pounds in with a litter of nine young ferrets and one jill. This was at eight o'clock in the morning. By two o'clock they had stripped every edible piece from the piglet. They are a constant source of worry to keep in good quality food at this age and are very expensive to keep. Most ferreters will part with them very cheaply at this age to avoid further expense, and I mean cheaply. The number sold at markets such as Bridgnorth and Penkridge in August for as little as twenty five pence will convince the buyer of the urgency of the breeder getting rid of his financially crippling litter of young ferrets. Unless one has a large pig or poultry farm nearby and losses are fairly high in these places, then breeding ferrets is a damnably expensive hobby. There was a time when I was easily able to get bags of day old chicks from hatcheries. These were battery house stock meant to lay in claustrophobia from six months old. The poultry sexers put down all the newly hatched male chicks and I had them as ferret food. Having seen battery houses and having my fear of enclosed spaces, I cannot help but feel that the dead males fed to my ferrets were the lucky ones. Now even this source has dried up as mink farmers and falconers snap up the supplies as soon as they are hatched. A story of the cost of rearing young ferrets will illustrate my point. Ernie Phillips, whom I mentioned earlier in my book *The Jack Russell* is a great ferreter and an even greater wit. In 1974 he reared a litter of twelve of the finest polecat kits I have ever seen; agile, healthy and pulsating with the same vitality as their owner (do ferrets get like their masters?). All our local hunters visited Ernie almost daily to view his splendid litter with envy. Mark and I arrived one Sunday to find the jill alone in the shed. "Sold 'em as a job lot for five bob each," said Ernie, who is still resisting the decimalisation of coinage with every fibre of his being. "Eating me out of house and home," he went on. "T'was either sell those or the nippers," he said, nodding at the seven year old twins, who were enacting Jack The Giant Killer scenes, slashing Mark's cactus dahlias with sharpened bed lathes. "Perhaps I made the wrong choice though," said Ernie as the last orange dahlia head hurtled across the garden. I for one could but question Ernie's wisdom in his choice of who to keep.

Livestock markets, in addition to being great fun, are also great sources of ferrets. Most small time ferret keepers bring their stock to sell at these places – for an advert "Ferrets for Sale" in the press often brings the planning department to the house on the grounds that you are conducting a business from a council house. A huge illegal building enterprise passes unnoticed, but a ferret breeder is a source of suspicion to tax man and planning department. I suppose the moral is "Never steal anything – small". I love the market, though I never buy anything from them. I listen with fascination to the lamping lurcher men who have brought in a host of illegally taken gutted rabbits to sell, the ferreters who have had yet another bad year at kit breeding and the dealers who will buy any form of livestock, stopping just short of dealing in the white slave trade. Here one can usually pick up a ferret at the end of August very, very cheaply, but beware, for there are snags. Firstly, this is indeed the classic case of buying a pig in a poke. Most ferrets are brought in nailed-down boxes and the only visible sign of a ferret is a nose or paw poking through a gap in the woodwork. Is it a hob or jill, a young one or a worn out old creature, fit only for a ferret knackers yard? Is it healthy, or is it the last of a litter expiring through sweats? Furthermore, even if the vendor uses a cage with a wire top you are hardly likely to see the beast at his best. Your seller places his goods on the table or stand with a brief note "one ferret hob – good worker" Then in comes a child with a cardboard box full of guinea pigs that he has outgrown and plonks them down next to the ferret. Another man puts a box full of tumbler pigeons on the other side, who are cooing contentedly unaware of the maddened ferret in the next cage who is thinking only of their grisly death and blood and feathers. Your ferret is now in a state of frenzy, so would you be surprised if you were bitten by a creature who is experiencing the hell of Tantalus. A child rattles his box roughly. "Come away, darling, they are nasty things," says snooty Mother on a day out to see how country folk sell their wares. Even the most gentle ferret will bite if picked up when faced with these tortures. So, if you will buy from markets, then for God's sake get your ferret home and let him settle before taking him out of the box. Moses Smith, my gypsy friend, who has a curious offbeat wisdom of his own, swears by these markets. He will wait at the entrance to a market for someone with a gingerly held box or writhing, cut-down sack, and question them. Mo is the most engaging of men so no one seems to get annoyed. If his victim is selling ferrets, Moses will ask to see them, handle them, pass an opinion on them. If Moses likes what he sees he will make the man an offer for his wares – always far too low, for like all gypsies, Moses feels insulted by anyone accepting his first offer. After convincing the man that the auctioneer's fee would knock a great hole in the ferret breeder's profit, Moses usually buys the ferrets and goes home with ferrets unruffled by the prodding of small children and the tantalising smell of its box mates. I confess that I do not have either Moses' nerve, or his great personal charm, so I leave market purchases strictly alone.

There are many commercial breeders of ferrets; Abbots of Thuxton, Norfolk, is one. These ferrets are usually fairly expensive if one considers the prices of the market as being the norm. Firms like Abbots usually have an amazingly varied collection of livestock and with a vast collection obviously a certain death rate – the cadavers finding their way to the ferret pens. I have seen ferrets bought from Abbot Bros and have nothing but praise for them. They have all been clean, healthy and extremely tame. Furthermore, they all have a condition that is hard to equal and almost impossible to better, so they are probably worth the extra price. Big breeders such as these usually try to keep up a good reputation, so if one is displeased with the ferret you have purchased, they will nearly always replace your ferret or refund the money. You have no such guarantee if you purchase a ferret down in some market; I confess I found my visit to Abbots fascinating. The jills rear their youngsters in individual cages, but the resulting young are run on in concrete-floored compounds with three feet high brick walls. These courts are replicas of the methods used in the middle ages. I saw maybe sixty ferrets in these courts and they all looked in excellent health. A trip to this firm is well worth the time.

Do not be impressed by adverts which state excellent working strain, as supplied to game keepers, foresters, etc. These ads sound impressive and make interesting reading, but they mean little. Ferrets are really only slightly domesticated polecats and so have lost little of their native instinct to hunt. All ferrets will work, and work well, if taken young and handled properly. Health and vitality is the important thing and strain is of little consequence. Good and bad ferrets are a result of good or bad management and training, and are not a result of genetic make up. One thing that is inherited, however, though before my talk with John Abbot I doubted this, is tameness or tractability. I saw Abbot reach into his ferret court and pull out a superb sandy hob without getting bitten. He assured me the hob had never been handled before. Still it is a good practise to handle one's ferrets frequently for the reasons I will discuss later on.

There are families or strains of very long, thin ferrets called greyhound ferrets, which were specifically bred for rat. They were of no specific colour, but they were simply slender ferrets. As a boy I saw them advertised frequently, but one rarely sees them for sale these days. I use my own for both rats and rabbits, and they (as will all properly handled ferrets) work both well.

Some form of club to eugenically promote the ferret (improve working strains) would perhaps be of use. Super hob ferrets could be put at stud and more important still, it could be used to give advice to beginners. I believe there is such a club in existence but I have not encountered it. The greatest use of this club would be to allow breeders to introduce new blood into their ferret stock, for inbreeding is very common in most districts and a variety of deformities are produced as a result of this badly planned genetic programme. However, I believe that eugenic improvement of the ferrets working ability to be unnecessary. Certain breeds of terrier, such as cairns, fox terrier, etc., have been ruined as work dogs because the show breeders have neglected to breed for working ability and have concentrated on appearance to the exclusion of hunting instinct. These breeds have become popular pets, not hunters. I do not see this happening to the ferret, though I had some doubts about this when myxomatosis made the ferret almost obsolete. I know of few ferret breeders who keep these animals as pets, and even the two pet keepers I know cannot resist trying their pets at the odd rabbit or rat now and again if the chance presents itself. There is little fear that the ferret will have the working instinct bred out of it in the next few thousand years, and by then the concrete juggernaut of the cities will have wiped out all wild life.

4 Housing

A rat or a rabbit is a natural athlete. He has access to natural foods, a chance to spar with his rivals and enemies and all the facilities to exercise its needs. If you wish to hunt with a ferret the least you can do is give the poor devil a chance to break even with its prey, even if it can't defeat him. You are asking a lot to put your ferret in a box that is a foot cube, feed him slop, and then take him out to do battle with a rat at least as big as itself and with almost as much fighting ability. This should be uppermost in the mind of the ferret keeper when he considers housing his ferret.

Well now you've bought your ferret. How are you going to keep him? The straight from the shoulder answer should be, in the biggest cage possible. The warreners of old kept them in enormous stone walled compounds called ferret courts where they could exercise, play and become very fit and lively. Modern man is not as claustro-phobic as his ancestors and as most of us live in little boxes our-selves, we tend to expect our livestock to live in similarly small pens. Today a dog can be kept (by law) in a kennel only just large enough for it to turn round in, and the owner will not be prosecuted if it can be proved that the poor creature is let out for just a while every day. Poultry are kept in battery houses that are horrendous to any person who is not totally agoraphobic. If you wish to keep your ferrets in such a place and in such conditions I wish you luck, for he or she will soon sicken and die. Ferrets need space.

To do your ferret justice he will need a large cage; 4′ × 2′6″ × 2′6″ is not too large. It allows him or her to climb, run about and get fit for the task for which they are intended – namely hunting. If he is unfit as a result of keeping him in cramped quarters then you will find him exhausted by a day's rabbiting, sometimes to the extent that he will refuse to enter the warren, but more often he will enter the hole willingly enough if only to find a dry place in which to rest. Even if one has a large cage it pays to allow your ferret a chance to run around the yard when cleaning out his cage – providing, of course, you do not keep chickens or similar edibles in the same yard. A man who keeps lamping lurchers (an illegal form of hunting using a lamp and a dog) will know by the gleam of his dog's coat when he is in first class condition. Likewise, a healthy ferret will dance and cavort about, encouraging his owner to chase it and play all manner of games with it. When a ferret hits this peak of condition he is more than ready to be matched against any rat or rabbit. Remember a large cage means much exercise, much exercise means good condition, and good condition means a good day's work. Furthermore, do remember a ferret in a small cage has difficulty keeping its meat clear of its dung corner and subsequently ingests food tainted with its own excreta. In a large cage a ferret will deliberately drag its meat away from its dung corner, but in a small cage it has no chance to do so – the result should be obvious.

I like cages constructed of tongue and groove wood. The wood can be quite thin, as ferrets are not rodents, so are unlikely to gnaw through the timber. The tongue slots neatly into the grove and prevents all draughts which are pretty nigh fatal to all animals. The sleeping compartment of a ferret cage, which can also be used for breeding kits, should be dark, warm and draught proof and should offer a degree of privacy to the creature. Try to remember that ferrets are descended from nocturnal creatures who slept through the day in secluded, dark places.

The run, which adjoins the sleeping quarters, should be made of fine mesh wire. Not only does this prevent a kit strewn out of the nest falling through the wire, but it also prevents a stray cat getting a paw through the cage front. This does sometimes happen. Mark Wibley, our local Midland raconteur, used inch wire netting in his ferret pen construction. One night Mark heard a racket that would have wakened the dead. He got out of bed and ran half naked down the path towards his ferret pen. (Not a pretty sight as Mark weighs over twenty stone.) A stray cat had just managed to get its tiny emaciated paw through the netting to get at a piece of sheep's paunch that Mark fed his ferrets. His ferret, a huge hob, as obese as its owner, had wakened and saw the paw as a vitamin supplement to the paunch diet and had seized it. The cat had clawed, screamed, kicked and writhed with pain. Now Mark was faced with a fascinating study in applied mathematics – how to separate one cat from one ferret and still leave one live, fat, man. Mark told this tale at one of the local pubs in Tamworth, and it lasted him all of three pints bought by admiring listeners. As we left, Ernie said "Old Mark is losing his grip. He made the same tale last five pints last week". Mark certainly hooked the summer visitors with his tales of ferreting and "man of the earth" exploits. It would have been a shame to tell them that he was a retired bank clerk.

Felt the roof of your tongue and groove shed. Avoid using galvanised iron like the plague, or aluminium for that matter. Felt will absorb some heat, but a galvanised roof will make your pen like an inferno in summer and an ice box in the cold days of winter. Also remember that a ferret is a meat eater. A rabbit's food will wilt in hot summer but still be edible, but a piece of meat, kept in a hot shed, will resemble a bacteriologist's dream in a matter of hours. Dr Henry Clamp is a local expert on ferret rearing, and he believes one can attribute many of the post nest deaths among kits to the fact that the sheds were overheated and the meat had gone slightly hot because of the temperature. Young kits die quite quickly from eating meat which is just slightly off. For this reason, if it is at all possible, put your ferret pens in the shade, out of direct sunlight. A hedge overhanging the cages provides shade and you will find your ferrets will improve greatly from this protection from bright sunlight.

There are many opinions on the construction of the floors of a ferret pen. Many breeders, particularly those who farm ferrets for their fur, use wire cages with wire floors, identical to the cages used for rearing mink. These are extremely hygienic, for the faeces and urine simply fall through the wire and the cages can be hosed out daily. Foot rot, that scourge of ferret breeders, is practically unknown in ferrets housed on wire floors – but such floors have their disadvantages. If a kit is thrown from the nest when the jill leaves to feed or to investigate a noise, then unless the wire of the floor is very fine, the kit will fall through. If the wire is very fine, however, it becomes clogged with faeces easily. These floors are also cold. I saw several jills reared under these Spartan conditions in Repton. They had very thick fur – they had to or die of exposure, but the fur lacked the lustre of ferrets reared in warm houses. Peter Robinson, our local mink farmer, bred several good healthy litters of ferrets in mink cages, but I have had little success using these methods. The mink has a very thick fur as a result of originating in the northern tundras of America and Asia where sub-zero temperatures are fairly common, and the cages of mink farms aim to simulate these freezing conditions in order to produce very thick-furred animals. Although wild polecats have been recorded at heights around 2,000 metres above sea level in alpine areas, it is not the creature of the tundra as is the mink. Hence it does not do well in very cold cages. Nor, therefore, does the domesticated polecat – the ferret.

A few weeks ago I noticed *Shooting Times* published an article on community breeding systems for ferrets. Here a large shed was utilised and bales of straw placed in strategic positions in the shed. The hob and jills were turned loose in this shed and allowed to breed at random. The author states that he had considerable success with this method with some jills deliberately stealing and adopting the young of the others. I would view this method with great suspicion and would certainly not use it. Firstly, it is unnatural – for wild polecats are solitary creatures and never lead communal lives. Even if two ferrets escape from my cage they never stay together but go their separate ways. The author mentioned that several young did disappear from various litters, but he attributed this to what he calls natural selection/culling. I would simply describe it as cannibalism brought about by overcrowding. A creature that is solitary by nature, placed in conditions of enforced communal breeding must suffer much mental strain. The young are born and the jill is protective towards them (just put your hand in a newly born litter and see the jill's reaction). She will be restless and disturbed by the approach of another jill. She will get up to guard her litter and her litter will be disturbed and squeal at the slight discomfort. Now ferrets, like all carnivores, clean the belly areas of young who squeal, to comfort them. If there are frequent interruptions by other jills there is frequent squealing by the young and subsequently frequent licking by the jill. The jill, now in a state of anxiety, licks frantically to stop the squealing and eventually draws blood at the umbilicus, or navel, of the kit, who squeals even more, but she has only one way to comfort him and licks and licks. In a matter of minutes the baffled and neurotic jill is cleaning and tearing out the entire guts from the abdominal cavity of the now frantically screaming kit. In the morning you will find a haunch or a head of what was yesterday a healthy ferret kit. Jills should be left in peace when they have their litters, for some will destroy an entire litter if upset – not to vent her spleen on her young, but merely as a result of anxiety brought about by being disturbed. I deplore community breeding for ferrets, though it must work for some people, but do these people ever stop to calculate the mortality rate in these litters? It must be alarmingly high. I believe that community breeding systems only work with animals whose ancestors were herd animals but I believe it causes awful psychological stresses among animals whose ancestors were solitary.

I know of few people who have any success with this method of community breeding. Henry Clamp, doctor, hunter and friend, allows his two jills and a hob to run together. All the year round they lived together, ate together and reared their young together, all in the same cage, which was about six feet long and two feet wide. I was sceptical when Henry told me he had reared satisfactory youngsters this way for several years. I was also very aware of Henry's veracity for he never pulled the long bow and never even exaggerated a hunting story. One day Henry asked me to his house, to see a goshawk we were going to fly at rabbit the next day. We passed his ferret cage and I asked casually about the youngsters. I think he saw the look of partial disbelief on my face. He opened the nesting compartment and saw two jills curled up suckling each other's youngsters. One litter was a week old, the other maybe nearly three weeks. Both jills suckled the litters at random. Henry threw a rabbit in the run, and in the scrabble, a week old youngster was thrown into the mesh-faced run. The hob, also tenant in the sleeping compartment, dashed out with both the jills and began to feed. The cold had now affected the kit, and it was squeaking loudly. What was more surprising was that the large, gentle, cream hob left the rabbit and carried the kit back to the sleeping compartment and then resumed his meal on the rabbit. If I had not seen this myself, then I would not have believed it. My own jills regard each other's youngsters as delicacies and if two are caged together and one kindles, then the other jill always eats them. Thus I always try to rear my youngsters by allowing a jill to kindle alone in her own cage that she has known for months. My litter average (reared) young ferrets, is higher than Henry's, so perhaps his sometimes do make mistakes. I certainly would not advise any person starting up in ferret breeding to try communal breeding methods. One jill, one cage, and live youngsters, would be my advice.

Getting back to housing, as I have stated, I dislike wire floors but I have seen some very satisfactory cages made by removing a piece of wood from the dung corner and tacking in some fine mesh wire which enables the dung to fall through to the earth. Similarly a sheet of steel, or aluminium, or simply an unrolled tin can, cut to fit into the dung corner is for easy cleaning and prevents the wood of the dung corner rotting. Ferret manure is very caustic, however, and not only rots wood rapidly, but will corrode steel and aluminium. Tom Evans gives a good tip for ferret cleanliness. Ferrets always defecate in the same corner even if the owner is stupid enough to allow a great pile of faeces to accumulate, then the ferret will add to it before it considers using another portion of the hutch. Tom used to leave a newly bought ferret in its carrying box for far longer than he need have. The ferret eventually defaecated in the corner of the carrying box. Tom would then gather up the faeces and smear them in the corner of the ferret cage that he regarded as most convenient for cleaning. Forever after the ferret obliged by fouling in that corner. It is a useful wrinkle when one considers the time taken in cleaning out a ferret cage where the occupant has decided to use an inconvenient spot.

I once saw an enormous pile of ferret dung, perhaps nearly a hundredweight, in the corner of a huge colony pen in Kirby. The pen was a huge galvanised affair with a concrete floor and a wire mesh front, and measured $25' \times 8'$. In the corner hung a huge sack and this was filled loosely with hay. At the sound of the door opening the ferrets cascaded from the sack in which they slept. The owner said that he cleaned them out once a year when he put them in the breeding pens and that he disinfected the pen with a blow lamp, left it for four months, and returned the jills and their litters to the pen later in the year. This was a method used by medieval warreners and has nothing to commend it. The stench is literally appalling, though I confess his stock looked well. Ferrets are protein eaters and are not very efficient at converting protein into ferret flesh. Hence the faeces are rich in unused protein and provide a superb breeding ground for housefly maggots. Furthermore, if ferrets are housed individually, and a disease such as mange breaks out, it is easily held in check. When such an infection breaks out in a colony (particularly where the faeces are rarely cleaned out) then it infects the whole batch in no time. Adult females thrive in some amazingly bad conditions, but the young are far more delicate.

The three golden rules of ferret housing should be:

Keep them clean.

Keep them dry and prevent draughts.

Keep them out of full sunlight which makes the pen hot, the food rank and the ferret dead.

5 Feeding

Let me begin this chapter by simply debunking a myth. Many ferret breeders swear by keeping their ferrets on a bread and milk diet and even rear litters on this slop mixture. The apparent logic behind this diet is that such a diet produces a ferret that has little or no instinct to kill underground. To anyone with half a brain, this argument does not hold water. Firstly, as I have explained, the ancestor of the ferret was the wild European polecat, which is a totally carnivorous animal. It is therefore very illogical to assume that just a few thousand years of domestication has produced an animal that has now developed a gut and alimentary system that can cope with a totally herbivorous diet with just a hint of animal protein in the milk. A ferret merely stays alive on a bread and milk diet, it does not thrive and the incidence of rickets and deformities through malnutrition in litters fed on such a diet is alarming. Still there are many bread and milk advocates who still breed and rear ferrets on this diet.

Having now, I hope, exploded the fallacy about a ferret's dietary needs let us now knock down the story that a slop fed ferret is unlikely to kill underground and lie upon its kills. Again, nothing could be further from the truth. One sometimes sees dogs eating their own excreta or the excreta of other dogs. This somewhat unpleasant complaint, incidentally referred to as pica or filth eating, is nauseating to us, but serves its purpose. Although most filth eaters devour faeces as purely a habit, the complaint probably had its origins in the fact that the dog craved for vitamins not found in its everyday diet but had sensed that they were present in the stools of other creatures. Animals, particularly rats, will do strange things to make up for the vitamins missing in their diets.

Now meat has an amazing number of vitamins in it, not just B_{12} as was thought by early scientists, but some so complex that dieticians are still discovering them so as to prepare man for a meatless future. These vitamins are simply not found in bread and milk.

The ferret now goes to earth to flush out a rat or a rabbit which is rich in the vitamins a ferret requires. If the creature fails to bolt, then the ferret kills it and finds itself surrounded by the vitamins it has been denied. It now crams itself with this rich food, deliberately overeating for the body now attempts to store the vitamins for the rainy day when the ferret returns to its bread and milk diet. The now overfull ferret has little inclination to leave its vitamin rich meal and, being overfull, it is drowsy and so lies up and sleeps on the warm carcase of its victim. The slop diet, far from discouraging the ferret from killing and lying up is probably the main cause of such failings. Hence, I hope I have exposed the second myth.

Obviously flesh is the answer to what to feed your ferret – and flesh it has to be if one is to rear a healthy ferret capable of a hard day's rabbiting or doing battle with a rat. Apart from shrews (which some ferrets will eat) stoats and weasels, there is practically no animal that a ferret will refuse to eat. All forms of butcher's meat is acceptable, though lights (lungs) tend to make the droppings a little fluid. Liver is greatly appreciated, in fact, mustelids of all kinds develop many maladies if denied the vitamins found in liver. Mink need daily supplies of liver to thrive, but ferrets are not so demanding.

Some years ago when man first began to understand his own dietary needs, a man called King, who was regarded as a crank by many, put forward an idea that many of man's modern ailments are due to the fact that he eats only selected pieces of the animals he kills, and that if man were to eat the whole carcase, then many of his aches and pains would go away. While I shudder at the thought of eating sheep's trachea and gall bladders, I believe King might not be such a crank as early people believe. I feed my ferrets whole carcases, never removing pieces, nor do I remove the carcase until the ferret has stripped it to bone, fur or feather (or in the case of a larger animal the body has become putrid). My ferrets are in excellent condition on this diet, which is exactly how his wild ancestor would have fed.

I belong to a group who are addicted to rat hunting, so we feed our ferrets loads of dead rats, fed whole and the ferrets eat up every scrap of these rodents except the tail and a few pieces of fur. Many people remove the tail of the rat before feeding as they believe that all the diseases of the rat are found in the tail. Rubbish, the whole of a rat's carcase is riddled with some very nasty bugs, such as

43

salmonella and Wiels disease. Curiously, Wiels disease, called lepto-
spiral jaundice in dogs, is an absolute killer to man and dog, yet I
have never seen a ferret show symptoms of this infection, even
though mine live for a good two thirds of their lives on the bodies
of rats. Rats are an excellent though perhaps unpleasant looking
diet, particularly for ferrets who are intended for rat hunting, for not
only are rats easily obtained, but their whole bodies are packed with
the vitamins that ferrets need. They are, in fact, a natural diet.
Furthermore, it must act as a boost to the ferret who goes rat hunting to know that the vicious little brawler who is fighting him is quite
delicious to eat. If you live in a built up area, then your neighbours
may not perhaps appreciate your feeding bags of rats to your ferrets,
but it is useful to allow your ferret to dine on a carcase or so at the
end of a day's hunt and to throw the remains of the rat away before
returning home.

I am also convinced that feeding rats helps the ferret's constitution when they are severely mauled by a rat during a hunt. The body
of a rat-fed ferret is now fairly used to the bacteria invading it via
the rat bites and has probably developed some antibodies to deal
with them. My own ferrets rarely fester after a rat bite, but a friend
of mine who abhors feeding rats to his ferrets invariably has septic
wounds on his ferrets after they have encountered a rat.

There are snags regarding feeding your ferrets on rats, however,
not just the fact that nosey neighbours will attribute every cold in
their children to an outbreak of Black Death. Beware of feeding
rats where Warfarin has been used. Warfarin is still deadly to most
rats, in spite of the alarmist columns of the national newspapers, who
say we are in for a super rat invasion (what on earth is a super rat?),
and a rat whose system is full of this deadly anticoagulant is certainly
not suitable food for your ferret. Some months ago I had a visit
from a friend of mine who brought with him a very apathetic,
"couldn't care less," jill ferret that had previously been a tiger on
rats. We worked out all possible illnesses and finally settled on the
fact that his ferret had dined on a rat probably dying of Warfarin
poisoning. Fortunately our diagnosis was correct, and out vet gave
it a series of Vitamin K injections to counteract the effects of the
Warfarin, and his ferret returned to its tigerish self. Another few days
untreated, however, and I feel he would have had a very dead ferret.
I always check as to whether any poison has been used around places
where I collect rats for ferret food. I also avoid picking up rat car-

cases from the road. Warfarin, as I have just mentioned, produces a doped, couldn't care less, attitude in its victim which makes them very vulnerable to traffic when they try to cross a road. Most of the rats squashed on roads, and one sees many, were probably stupified by some poison before the vehicle hit them. If you are in any doubt about the reason for the death of the rat, don't feed it. Feed only healthy, fresh rats that your dogs or ferrets have killed.

Rabbits are a different matter. Any scraps, waste, guts, heads etc., of rabbits or hares are perfectly acceptable and very safe food for your ferret and although no ferret will eat the contents of a rabbit's stomach, the rest of the entrails are greatly enjoyed. Myxied rabbits, even in the last stages of the disease, make excellent ferret food, for the disease is confined only to rabbits and will not harm your ferret, dog or cat; nor you for that matter. I once lived for several weeks on the carcases of myxied rabbits and suffered no ill effects. Ferrets certainly do not mind eating them. The guts of the rabbit are invariably festooned with tape worms but I have never found tapeworm segment in my ferrets dung corner, so I suspect that this particular species of tapeworm only infects the rabbit.

One of my favourite anecdotes about feeding ferrets occurred when I was living in a particularly seedy district of the north country. I lived in a typical two up, two down, run down house, and such districts are characterised by two features: (a) the houses seldom have gardens, so my ferrets lived in the murky little backyard, and I confess in my outside toilet, (b) these districts are inhabited by the most nosey people it has been my misfortune to meet. At that time I supplemented my pathetic salary as a teacher by poaching rabbits and lecturing to various intellectual clubs on British Mammals, mostly foxes, which were, and are, a particular interest of mine. One night, at one of these lectures, I met the woman of my dreams, for not only was she glamorous and bright, but she worked for a firm of livestock importers and could procure me vast quantities of exotic carcases for my ferrets. From then on my ferrets dined like Persian potentates, lanner falcons, finches, flamingoes and a variety of parrots, who gave me the shudders about contracting psittacosis, graced my ferrets' menus. Monkeys were their staple diet, for colds, chills and shock must kill hundreds of the poor devils when they reach this country. At that time I lived next door to a woman my friends had dubbed four times winner of the Nobel prize for being the most nosey woman in the world. Every visitor to my house

45

brought a slight movement from her lace curtains. We were a rowdy crowd and she probably had good reason to complain to the council, who visited us so often we set aside a special mug for the council official's tea. Then, one day, we had a visitor of a different kind. I opened the door and a man produced a card with a speed and flourish that would have put a professional conjurer to shame – police. He pushed past me, eyed my curious friends, and walked straight to the backyard, pausing to say in a menacing tone that he had had complaints. He eyed my ferret cage intently. A dead rhesus monkey face, stripped of flesh, but one paw intact, lay in the cage. Our CID man had stopped looking like Kojak and now had a slightly sheepish look on his face. It appeared that our neighbour had seen the partly eaten monkey from her side of the fence and had reported me for feeding a stillborn or newly born coloured baby to the ferrets. It was a subject of jokes for weeks. Whenever we went out we shouted comments about our night's grave robbing exploits, noisily banging our spades to confirm her fears. One of our group went too far however, for he persuaded a fool to visit her house saying that he was from the amputation department of the local hospital and as he could obtain no answer next door, could he possibly leave the pieces with her. Strangely, a few weeks later, she left and went to live with her sister in Doncaster. A month later I left the district and I am told my departure was greeted with sighs of relief by the community. My way of life did not suit the district, I'm afraid.

We still feed stillborn kittens and puppies to our ferrets, for we have some losses from my kennels and catteries, but if a creature lives a few days and then fails to thrive, we bury or burn the carcases. The chances are that it is infected with some deadly malady like hepatitis which can do damage to ferrets. Stillborn or premature animals are usually quite safe to feed, however. I once lost nearly all my batch of ferrets through feeding a dead three week old puppy to my ferrets. Yes, it had died of distemper and you can guess the rest. Some of my friends pick up road casualty cats and feed them to their ferrets – probably highly illegal but I doubt whether any magistrate's court would make a case if it was to be brought to court. This again is not without dangers for few people inject street moggies against cat diseases, such as feline infectious enteritis which is not only a real killer to cats, but can also wipe out a batch of ferrets within a few days. By feeding a dead roadside cat you may well be bringing the deadliest disease of all into your ferretry. Leave roadside cat casualties strictly alone. Rabbits, hedgehogs (who have never come to terms with motor cars and die in thousands) make excellent food if fresh and can usually be picked up on any country road. Most bird casualties are also gratefully accepted by ferrets.

An excellent standby, should one's hunting or search for automobile victims prove to be fruitless, is sheep's paunch or cow tripe. It is cheap, usually very easily obtainable, and if hung up individually on nails, lasts a fair time without getting very rank. This food lacks quite a lot of essential vitamins, so your ferrets will need a whole carcase once in a while, but as a fairly constant staple diet such paunches and tripes are hard to beat. In times when I fail to obtain rats, my own ferrets are fed on these.

At one time, to eke out my meagre grant in college, I worked for a fishmonger/poulterer whose business was on the way out because of bad management and his love of whisky. He was big, Irish and good humoured and when I mentioned that his "bottle a day" habit was causing hardening of his liver, he promised me the said organ on his death to use as leather for the soles of my shoes. I was given the chicken offal for the ferrets and, though they thrived on it, it went rank very quickly and stank dreadfully. Poultry heads are often suspect food as they are sometimes the heads of capons – cock birds sterilised by injecting a pellet of stilboestrol into the head or neck of the cockerel. This chemical caused the sexual organs to atrophy and the energy of the bird was directed into making extra flesh. Mink farmers fight shy of feeding these heads, or indeed any poultry offal to their stock, as there are usually still traces of stilboestrol left in the head and this is reputed to make male mink impotent and to cause the females to abort. As a matter of interest, this same chemically produced hormone is used to bring reluctant Siamese female cats into season. Curiously, although I fed the heads of both capons and unsterilised fowl to my ferrets, I found no ill effects. One scientist in America suggested that American manhood would be made impotent by ingesting this chemical in the table poultry. When tests were done it was proved he was right, providing one could eat 700 poultry heads a day. I do not believe these traces of stilboestrol, and they are only minute traces by the time the bird is ready for slaughter, have very much effect on any mammal, though a friend of mine noted that his male goshawk developed female plumage after he fed the bird capon heads. I am tempted to question whether or not the bird would have done the same had my friend not fed the heads.

47

To my mind the only danger of feeding these heads and bowels is the fact that unless frozen the offal goes bad very quickly and the putrefaction causes toxic chemicals which, though they do not harm older ferrets, are fatal to young kits just leaving the nest.

Fish waste is not usually taken very willingly by ferrets at first, but after a short fast they will eat it readily enough. There is an old wives' tale that any form of salt is fatal to a ferret (curious as blood is very salty). This is still believed by many hunters in the Midlands to this day. I fed waste mackerel, cod, halibut, plaice and God knows what, but I experienced no problem with feeding them this fish which must have had a high salt content. Fish goes bad quickly, however, and should be fed with care. I experienced one other problem with fish feeding – the stench from the dung of flesh-fed ferrets is bad, but the smell from the dung corner of ferrets fed on fish was unbelievable. As I lived in a very built up area, I stopped feeding the fish.

Just as polecats are said to put away frogs for a rainy day, so should the ferret keeper lay up stocks for a rainy day when food is scarce. If one has a deep freeze, then there is no problem, – one of my friends even freezes down rats after a hunt (no, he uses the freezer strictly for animal food, not for human foodstuffs) – though ferrets sniff de-frosted meat carefully before eating. Perhaps their delicate nostrils can detect some chemical change in frozen flesh that our own micro-analysis tests cannot. Anyway, ferrets seem to know if meat has been frozen. If one does not have a deep freeze then greaves or dried meat is a useful standby. This is meat which has been heat dried and has lost most of its water. Greaves needs soaking in boiling water overnight before feeding. Most ferrets will gnaw unhappily at unsoaked meat. As I have stated, greaves is a useful standby, though for the first few days of feeding it causes bad diarrhoea. I know many breeders who feed only greaves and rear satisfactory litters, but I do not believe it is anywhere near as good as raw bloody meat. It will however keep indefinitely if kept dry so is valuable in this respect.

If one intends to keep many ferrets you will develop the instincts of a vulture. You will learn almost instinctively where some livestock disaster has taken place and will be on the doorstep to collect the bodies. You will find yourself fighting all manner of inner conflicts with yourself during a thunderstorm, for you know that the turkey farm in your village will have many fresh and free cadavers when the frightened birds crowd on top of each other killing the bottom layer of turkeys. A power cut will find you at the battery houses collecting birds which have suffocated when the fans fail. Myxomatosis, a curse in itself, will yield you many carcases of weak and dying rabbits, all very acceptable to your ferrets. You will be regarded by farmers as a bird of ill omen. Mark once said that a black shroud and a scythe should be my trade mark, but after a while farmers and livestock keepers will phone you to fetch fallen animals to save them the trouble of burying them. You will cease to be regarded as a human pariah, a rifler of graves and will be regarded as a useful, though scavenging, member of the countryside. Tom Cope, our local farmer and owner of the famous Huddlesford herd of Friesian cattle, once said I occupied the same position in Huddlesford as did the hyena in Africa. A doubtful compliment, but I keep my ferrets very cheaply.

As I have stated, polecats were originally water loving animals, rarely straying far from streams. It is commonsense therefore to ensure that ferrets have a good supply of fresh water at all times. They will annoy you sometimes by splashing and tipping their water bowls, but you must put up with this annoyance and replenish their dishes. All carnivorous animals need large amounts of water to wash out wastes from the protein they eat. To keep a ferret short of water is just asking for trouble.

6 Breeding

Losses among ferrets used for hunting are usually quite high – ferrets die from both cat and dog diseases, succumb to most types of coli infections, die as a result of rat bites and sometimes, when rabbiting, lie up and get lost. Therefore, if you intend to hunt regularly you will need to breed a considerable number of ferrets to replace the casualties. This, however, is not the only reason for breeding ferrets. Most veterinary surgeons will usually advise dog owners to breed from a bitch perhaps just once during her lifetime, as bitches often develop all sorts of gynaecological disorders if not allowed to have puppies. Ferrets are far worse in this respect. Many, but not all, jill ferrets will come into season early in the year and remain in this condition for many months unless mated. This has a damaging effect on the constitution of the ferret, and many simply fade away and die if denied motherhood. Some develop feminine diseases such as pyometra and metritis, and these are fatal if not treated. So if you have a jill it is more than just advisable to breed from it.

You will have no doubt when your jill is in season. Watch out from February onwards. The vulva begins to swell and get very pink. Sometimes a whitish discharge is passed from the vagina. Your jill is now ready to mate. Place her in the hob's cage. At first he will sniff at her and the pair will run around chattering. Suddenly the hob will seize the back of the jill's neck viciously, dig in his teeth, hoist himself on her back and with one pelvic thrust push his penis into her vagina – all the time tightening the grip on the back of her neck. He will lie in this position for up to an hour – most of the time the jill screaming as though he were mangling her to death. Many tyro ferret keepers fear for the ferret's life and rush in to stop the hob which they believe is killing their jill. Do not interfere with them, for all mustelids mate in this seemingly savage manner. It is believed that mustelids cannot conceive unless they indulge in this barbarous and savage courtship. Some scientists believe that the female cannot ovulate unless she is bitten around the neck. I believe this to be true – I once borrowed a superb white hob from a friend of mine. He was an incredible line ferret, and a first class worker. He lay on the female, put in the pelvic thrust and did not grip the back of the neck of any of the jills he served. At first I treated this with simply mild curiosity but I noticed that as the year went on his jills still stayed in season. I put them with another hob who savagely bit their necks as he mated, and they became pregnant. Often a young, over-eager hob will mangle the back of a jill's neck until it resembles a blood stained pulp, for young hobs will endeavour to serve a jill every few hours of the day. They are also very active at night as the nocturnal screams and cries will indicate. Again expect strange glances from the neighbours who will wonder what is going on. If a hob is far too over eager, remove the jill after he has served her and replace her once a day. I have a dark polecat hob so violent that I cannot leave him in with the jills for long, yet he breeds litters of twelve as a result of his sadistic courtship. As soon as the jill has conceived, the vaginal swelling will subside. If the male loses interest in her, leave her with him awhile – it will do no harm, but if the male is young and lusty and still pesters the female repeatedly by trying to mate her, then it is best to remove her to another cage.

Within a matter of a few weeks the swollen and bloody area around the jill's neck will subside and towards the fifth week after mating a bright new patch of fur appears. If one finds a stray jill with this new patch of fur then you can put her in a separate cage for she has been mated and is probably in kindle. I found such a jill a week or so ago and she has produced a litter.

Keep your mated jill away from the hob, feed her her normal diet, or maybe even a bit less than usual until she is about four weeks pregnant and then slightly increase the food. Do not feed an ad lib diet throughout the pregnancy for she will usually produce large foetuses which are difficult to give birth to, and the exhausted jill sometimes dies in parturition. It is better to keep her slightly short of food during pregnancy than to over feed. Look at it logically. In the wild a pregnant polecat is slowed up on account of the fact she is carrying an extra burden in the form of her unborn litter. Thus she is likely to make fewer, not more, kills and subsequently her body makes allowances for this slowing up of hunting rate and utilises the available food more efficiently – thus the ad lib method of feeding during pregnancy is unnatural and dangerous. As the reader will have gathered, I try to treat my ferrets as nature would treat a wild polecat. Allow a pregnant jill ferret to overeat all through her pregnancy and the chances are that the young will be so big as to present a problem in delivery and will be born dead or more than likely, damaged, so that the upset jill eats them.

As the jill gets more pregnant, say five weeks after her mating, it is time to stop hunting her. True, the foetus of a predatory animal is very well buffered against the bumps and knocks of hunting, but the jill's unborn litter will not improve through a severe kicking by a doe rabbit. Nor will her foetuses benefit from the sepsis introduced from a severe mauling from a rat. I have seen several litters born premature and dead after the pregnant jill has been badly mauled by a rat. So do not work a pregnant jill. Let her out for exercise, but do not allow her to jeopardise her litter by hunting her.

The gestation period of a ferret is between six and seven weeks, and towards the fifth week she will look obviously pregnant. Most of the year we bed our ferrets on fresh, clean, shavings which absorb the smell, are easy to clean out and smoulder slowly, burning away any faeces mixed with them. However, when the jill is five weeks pregnant it is wise to throw a large handful of soft hay, dried grass, or suchlike, in her nesting compartment. As the jill nears her time of kindling she will make a rough nest of this material and bury herself in the bedding. In this rough nest she will give birth to her kits. Avoid disturbing her now. A cat passing over the top of her cage is enough to make excitable young jills anxious, and the result of this anxiety is an eaten litter. Other jills, however, are so phlegmatic as to allow the breeder to watch the birth of the kits without the jill being in the slightest bit distressed. Be on the safe side however, and do not disturb the jill. Some young and inexperienced jills often have their litters born outside the nest – one of mine gave birth to a litter in her freshly cleaned out dung corner. Obviously if these are allowed to remain there then she will lose many as they will chill easily – particularly an early litter born in March. Do not despair. Take out the jill and place her on the ground, giving her a saucer of milk to occupy her time and attract her interest. While she is drinking, move her young into the nest. After a moment or so replace the jill and she will usually settle in the nest. Some jills are admittedly so neurotic that they will murder their young at the smallest excuse, but most will accept the move from inconvenient corner to nest without complaint. Some countrymen go through an elaborate ritual before handling a new born litter – rubbing their hands in the jill's faeces corner before picking up a kit. This, they believe, removes the scent of man. A nasty practice, but also a little pointless, for if you handle your ferrets often, then her pen will have traces of your scent anyway, so the muck smearing practice is not really essential.

Now reader, beware, for on having young the tamest jill will react with almost mad ferocity to protect her young. She will even fly at your hand and bite when you replenish her water bowl, or bring in her food. Your lamb is now a lion and believe me, a ferret with young is often a formidable force to reckon with and many an inexperienced ferreter who has taken all manner of liberties with his jill finds that she can be extremely ferocious when she has young. Treat your newly kindled jill with respect or she will teach you the error of your ways. A story will again illustrate my point. When I moved to this district I made most of my living from selling netted rabbits, and used one small polecat jill who was a great bolter, and so tame that if my friend was on the other side of the hedge and I wanted the jill, he would throw her and I would simply catch her. It never occurred to her to bite. She was indeed a treasure. I could also take food from her mouth and take all manner of liberties with her. I mated her to my old sandy hob – a veteran with one eye bitten out by a rat who had lodged in a rabbit warren, but had paid dearly for his lodging. She produced her litter of nine three days premature. One morning I opened her cage to play with her, for she would roll on her back like a kitten when I tickled her. She emerged from her nest quite quickly and put five rapid, sharp, nips in my fingers. It was only then that I realised that she had had her litter. She struck at my hand with the speed of a cobra, just hard enough to draw blood and to warn me not to interfere with her litter. She was a changed animal now she had taken on the responsibility of child rearing.

After five or six days, a litter of apparently healthy youngsters sometimes suddenly dies and the keeper/countryman/poacher whispers the dreaded word "sweats", for any unaccountable death is explained by this all-enveloping term. This is rubbish, for the litter deaths are not to do with any disease, but due to a hormonal imbalance, for if the jill with the now dead litter is examined, you will find that she has come in season again, and the body, baffled by the hormone upset prepares itself for mating by stopping the production of milk. The young have quite simply starved to death. Put her to the hob and she will mate immediately and with luck you will have a healthy litter next time. When I first noticed this phenomena I attributed it to the feeding of capon heads which contain stilboestrol and bring ferrets, cats and dogs in season. I now no longer believe this, for it is either just one of nature's mistakes, or the jill had had some chemical warning inside her system that the litter were not thriving and that the only way to continue her bloodline was to come in season again and produce a healthy litter. I have seen this phenomena happen several times, even with breeders who do not feed poultry waste. You will usually have no trouble with her next litter. The sexual cycles of all mustelids are all a bit of a mystery.

You may be surprised to see that the young ferret is born blind, naked, and very helpless. They grow fairly quickly and by about twenty days old they will avidly suck at meat brought to the nest by the dam. They are still totally blind at that age, as are young polecats, and for exactly the same reason. At thirty to thirty six days old their eyes open and they begin to explore the cage with a strange look of utter bewilderment. Curiously, as soon as the young's eyes open, the jill's resentment at their being handled totally ceases. Most baby kits at thirty to thirty six days old will hiss and spit at the breeder and even go through the motions of trying to bite, though the carnasial teeth are sharp, the jaw lacks the strength to inflict even a skin breaking bite. Handle them regularly as soon as the jill ceases to resent your touching them. This is indeed the first step in making a ferret tame. Unlike Abbot Brothers, I believe that it is this handling that produces tractability and gentleness – though I confess that my visit to Abbot Brothers did much to knock my ideas on the head.

Sadly the period of thirty six days onwards is usually the time when the greatest mortality occurs in ferrets, for as soon as the young begin to leave the nest, it is the time when certain breeders lose quantities of youngsters. Whole litters are wiped out at this time. My friend, Jeff Elwood, once fed his litter of eight healthy young polecat and white ferrets, all eagerly awaiting feeding, before he went to work that morning. They displayed the usual symptoms of good health, racing around the pen and climbing the wires as if they had been starved – all excellent signs of good health. All was well and Jeff went off to work. When he rattled the cage next morning, a jill (the mother) came to the wire and nothing else. At first Jeff suspected thieves, but on opening the nesting compartment he found seven dead kits and one rapidly on the way out. Jack Legge, who does much vermin control in the Midlands, reported an identical happening the very same week of Jeff's disaster. Both adult jills were intact and healthy. The poacher/game keeper/countryman again whispers the dreaded word "Sweats", or "ferret distemper", for the disease is so lethal and frightening to a ferret keeper, that all deaths are attributed to this malady, for once a person has experienced this plague, it is so heartbreaking that any outbreak of unexplainable disease is attributed to it. I suppose this attitude is very understandable when one considers the misery a killing disease brings the livestock owner. I suppose that after the Black Death ravaged Britain a person had only to sneeze in the street for the population to consider the total evacuation of a town. It is obviously not sweats that caused the death of both these litters, for an outbreak of canine distemper would not only have wiped out the litter, but seen off the adult jills as well. I was frankly fascinated in these deaths, which from now on I shall refer to as post-nest deaths. This post-nest death rate is probably almost as high in polecats living and breeding wild, and is probably nature's way of ensuring that the predatory population does not get out of hand. But although this may be true, it gives little consolation to the ferret keeper who finds his litter of healthy youngsters die overnight. Subsequently I decided to devote a great deal of time to finding out the reason for these post-nest deaths and I shall discuss my findings in my chapter on diseases.

Now is the time to make pets of your young ferrets. Forget the fool who handles his ferrets with thick gloves and states that ferrets have to be savage to hunt. Dismiss also the theories of the man who states that it is bad to hunt rats with ferret as it makes the ferrets savage. Encourage your ferret kits to play with your fingers, tickle their undersides, treat them as you would a litter of puppies or kittens, and play all manner of games with them. If you have well behaved children allow them to play with them and carry them about. A well behaved child will certainly not be bitten by a young ferret unless the child really hurts it. I have a close friend whose four year old child plays with his young ferrets as a child would play with toy soldiers. One elderly school teacher who came to the house was horrified as she had read the grossly exaggerated

Correct method of holding a ferret.

short story, Shredni Vashtar – the huge hob that a lonely child had willed to kill his cruel aunt. The child stood far more chance of being bitten by the schoolmistress's toy poodle. Another way of gentling young kits (and also an essential part of the training) is to allow them to drink milk from the palm of one's hand. Place drops of milk in the palm of your hand and allow the ferret to drink. Give every jill and hob in the litter a chance to see that the human hand can give good things and is not just an implement that snatches them up roughly and places them in a box or bag. I believe this prevents the dreaded fault known in the Midlands as skulking, where a ferret pokes his head just out of the earth and goes back into the hole every time the human hand reaches for it. I am convinced that this habit, which is damned nigh impossible to break when it is firmly established in the ferret, is a result of snatching up the ferret, or hurting it in some way during its early training. If the young ferret regards the human hand as a source of good things like milk and affection, it is unlikely to want to skulk but comes out to investigate what the hand has to offer. Never break the bond of friendship between man and ferret by rough handling.

Get young ferrets used to being put in travelling boxes or bags before actually being taken hunting. Any pigeon trainer gets his birds accustomed to being put in a basket for a few minutes a day before sending them on their first training flight. A ferret placed in his travelling box or bag frequently is not faced with the somewhat bewildering experience of being boxed up, put in a motor car, hear the engine rev up, arrive at its destination, taken out of its box and thrust down a rabbit hole for the first time in its young life. A ferret so treated must, to say the least, appear to be a little confused. There is much difference of opinion on the relative merits of carrying ferrets in boxes or sacks. Firstly, if ferrets are carried in individual carrying boxes, one ferret to one box or compartment, then each lid can be opened separately and the ferret taken out without the rest swarming all over the place. If you favour multiple boxes, which I hate, then it is a nightmare to get one ferret out without the rest also desperately making a bid for liberty. Boxes are hot, however, even if fairly well ventilated, so leave unused ferrets in the shade when out hunting, for ferrets go down fairly readily with heat stroke.

Sacks, I suppose, are convenient to carry, easy to dispose of and

A useful carrying bag for one or two ferrets.

A converted and ventilated ammunition box makes an excellent carrying box for a single ferret.

hung from one's belt while ferreting. Some ferrets are regular Houdinis at scratching through them and escaping, however. I had one sandy hob who could not be kept in a sack and did a fair amount of damage to one rather fragile carrying box I once made. I eventually gave him away to an unsuspecting hunter, who finally carried him in a steel ammunition box. Sacks are usually cooler than carrying boxes however, and do not need to be ventilated. Most ferreting, however, is done in winter, so it must also be pointed out that sacks are colder. For the beginner I should advise buying a carrying box from a reputable firm and forget about carrying bags and sacks.

As I have stated, colour is not important in a ferret, but during the breeding season I get inundated by enquiries about what would happen if someone crossed a white with a sandy, or how does one breed a really dark fitch ferret, so I have drawn up a chart that will tell the colour breeder all he wants to know. It is a pointless chart as white ferrets work as well as sandies or polecats, but it will, perhaps, prevent the misery of answering the million summer phone calls on what colour ferret one can expect by crossing a so and so with a so and so.

Colours to Expect

Mating	White	Sandy	Fitch
Fitch × Fitch	Sometimes	Sometimes	Almost certainly
Sandy × Fitch	Sometimes	Sometimes	Almost certainly
Sandy × Sandy	Sometimes	Sometimes	Never
White × Sandy	Sometimes	Sometimes	Never
White × White	Always	Never	Never

7 Hunting

"Now, this is a two holed warren, Brian. I'm going to put this hob in one hole and the rabbit will bolt from the other. When it does, hit it with a stick." I was eight years old, excited and took everything Tom said as serious. In went the hob, bump went the earth and out flashed the rabbit. I swung my stick at it, missing it by thirty yards, and looked back sadly at Tom. It was the first time I had ferreted and the first time I had ever seen a ferreted wild rabbit. I felt slightly ashamed of my efforts. "Even when you are a grown man," said Tom, "you will never be fast enough to do that. So if you do not learn to place your nets properly you will have no chance of catching your rabbit." What an educationalist Tom would have made! He needed the money for that rabbit, but was prepared to lose the rabbit to explain a point to a child. Do they make people like that these days? I doubt it.

The rabbit is not a native of Britain, the Romans probably brought over a few pairs and, rabbits being rabbits, they did the rest by themselves. In medieval times villages kept full time warreners on their staffs, just as they employed smiths and armour makers. His job was to make sure that the rabbit population never got so high as to endanger the villagers strips of land being denuded of crops. They were also used to provide some of the food for the table of the lord of the manor and also for the serfs, for contrary to the Robin Hood type legends, the taking of rabbits by common folk did not result in acres of peasants hanging from the Sheriff's gibbet. Right up to the industrial revolution the illegal taking of rabbits was never regarded as a serious offence. On the continent it was different, however, and I have often thanked God for that strip of water called the English Channel.

Prior to the outbreak of myxomatosis in this country, the rabbit could be a very serious pest. Rabbits are not rodents, they belong to a related group known as lagomorphs, but they have roughly the same breeding habits as rodents, and are just about as prolific as mice, rats and voles. By the time the doe is five months old she is ready to breed. She mates and after a gestation period of thirty one days she produces a litter of up to twelve young – though about six seems to be the average size of a litter. Now a curious fact about lagomorphs and rodents is that within an hour of producing a litter, the doe can mate again and conceive. Subsequently from the time a doe is five months old to the time when winter frosts bring a cessation of the breeding cycle, the doe is always pregnant. There is an elaborate survey being conducted on the continent into the phenomena called super foetation – a term which means the animal can carry two litters at different stages of development. It is a phenomena known, or I should say believed, to be present in the brown hare. Whether or not it appears in the rabbit is a point to be investigated. I very much doubt if it does. I am sure that commercial rabbit breeders who produce forty youngsters from a single doe, would have discovered it and certainly capitalised on it. Whether or not it occurs is not really important. The wild rabbit is prolific enough without this added boost to breeding. When winter sets in the doe rabbit either becomes infertile, or refuses to mate, so no young are usually born in winter. In 1975 however, the winter was so mild that the rabbits did breed right through the winter months. In the district near my cottage I had "scuttlers" a term for baby rabbits small enough to get through a purse net bolting as early as February 1st. It is said that the rabbit's breeding cycle is brought about by the temperature of the air rising. Commercial rabbit breeders keep their rabbitries warm, and though some does are reluctant to breed during winter, most will breed the whole year round if the sheds are warm. Certainly a mild winter means early youngsters and early youngsters mean all manner of problems for the ferreter, but I will deal with these later.

I doubt whether a great deal of research has been done on the rabbit's life span. Locksley's book *The Private Life of The Rabbit*, an informative, cleverly written, though not particularly exciting book, mentions most of the rabbit's habits, but omits to mention the life span. As a boy I knew a youth in my village who kept a tame buck rabbit for thirteen years, but I doubt whether a wild rabbit will live longer than two or three years in the wild. Creatures which have a high rate of breeding, usually have a correspondingly short life span. I know of one rabbit, however, who led a solitary and charmed life on the edge of a fashionable estate in Lichfield.

The poor beast had been hemmed in by the groups of £14,000 boxes being built where once green meadows had existed. He alone had survived. He was quite solitary and still alive after three years. At first people thought of a wild rabbit in their garden as having a quaint extra urban charm, but when dahlias, beans, sprouts and sundry edibles were nibbled to the ground, then he was no longer a novelty. He just had to go. Mark's huge hulk levered itself out of his tiny Fiat one morning and asked to borrow help and some nets. Mark spent hours showing drink-buying townies the art of net making and they looked excellent. The only problem was they didn't work. I used to buy top grade nets from proper net making companies and they always did work. Hence Mark's rural craft centre project was only viable because it brought him drink buying customers. He dared not sell one of his ghastly nets for fear of reprisals from his customers/victims. We set out for Lichfield, quickly located the warren, a simple two holed affair, and put in a hob ferret. Wham – our net was filled with one ancient rabbit. Normally when I kill a rabbit, I do not gut him near the warren for fear of alarming those still underground – a good tip this, but there was no rabbit within two miles so I set to work to skin the old rabbit then and there. I take roughly a minute to skin and gut a freshly killed rabbit for the pelt comes off easily when the rabbit's body is warm. Not so with this one, the skin was anchored to the flesh with manicles of ancient fibre. Five minutes later I finished the job. "You are not going to eat this, are you, Mark?" I said. "Of course," said Mark, giving me an almost contemptuous look. Two nights later we met Mark in his Tamworth pub. He had his usual crowd of drink buying admirers, and our asking for culinary advice on cooking a senile rabbit was well worth someone buying him another drink. "The art of cooking any ancient game," he said, sipping his whisky, "is a simple one to any true countryman." (Mark was born in Ealing.) "Firstly add your rabbit to the boiling water and insert a steel axe head. Boil for a considerable time (the crowd of admirers had increased to twenty) and when the axe head is soft and tender, the rabbit will be ready in another ten minutes." Curiously there were people ready to take in his crazy tale. I digress, however, from my study of the rabbit.

Tom Jones, poacher and naturalist of Lichfield, believes that rabbits rarely wander far from the warrens where they were born and that localised varieties exist. Tom boasts he can tell from which area a rabbit was caught by its fur colour and texture of pelt. From my knowledge of Tom I would not doubt his ability. This existence of localised varieties may be due to two factors:

(a) that inbreeding brought about by roads and traffic inhibiting migration does produce distinct features in isolated strains;

(b) that domestic rabbits do escape and bucks by dint of their extra size and strength serve many does in the district where they have escaped. The resulting offspring mate together and produce distinctly different types of rabbits from the rabbits of the ordinary countryside. Some years ago I was given a silver fox rabbit to look after by a young boy who was going on holiday. To my dismay it escaped. I paid the lad a sum of money to staunch the flow of tears and forgot about it. A few weeks later I saw the rabbit in the headlights of my car, but it was now too wild to catch. I saw him several times in the next few months, then he just disappeared. Five years later I bolted two wild young rabbits into my nets; both were coloured like the lost, and probably long dead, silver fox. The old escapee had left his mark on the population.

During the pre-war years, and perhaps up to 1950, rabbits were the noted pest of the farming community. Vast areas of land were laid waste by them, but then came the answer to the rabbit problem. One of nature's hellish control methods reinforced and cultivated by man. English or European rabbits imported to South America quickly died of a sickening malady, whereas the wild South American rabbit – a slightly different species – seemed unaffected by the disease. Something clicked in the mind of some scientist cum pseudo-naturalist, that the reason was that the South American bunny carried a bug to which it was immune, but was deadly to the European species of rabbit. A slight cold in Britain was taken to Greenland by a ship's crew and wiped out several Eskimo villages. The bug that slew the English rabbit was finally isolated and used to kill several innocent laboratory rabbits, before being released on an estate in France, for the landowner had all he could take of rabbits. It spread like wild fire through the rabbit population of France. Normally the English Channel would have stopped this bug, but there were many English landowners who were also quite keen to reduce the rabbit population of their English estates. There is no doubt that the disease was deliberately introduced into Britain, either by bringing diseased rabbits, or rabbit carcases, or perhaps, more sinister still, by importing vials of the actual virus. Anyway, myxomatosis had arrived in Britain and was here to stay.

As with the French rabbit, our own had no immunity to this sickening disease, and died in the millions. It was a common sight to see dozens of crippled, blinded, rabbits along the sides of the road or sitting in the middle of the road quite impervious to the passing traffic – all just waiting to die. Many landowners, where the disease had not touched, gave good prices for myxied rabbits to introduce onto their own land to curb their own rabbit problem. To my great shame and disgrace, I once supplied a batch of these diseased rabbits to a landowner, for at that time no one quite realised the virulence of the bug. The myxomatosis virus is spread from rabbit to rabbit by a particular type of rabbit flea which was found in virtually every burrow, so there was no escape. True, some rabbits, by happy accident, bred above ground and survived, for they had no contact with the flea. Some rabbits however became immune to the virus, for not every human died when infected with even the Black Death. Those who developed the infection while carrying young usually died as did non pregnant does, but those who did survive passed on some immunity to their young in the colostrum or first milk. There were damnably few who survived the first impact of the disease however.

The rabbit disaster, for every decent person must surely regard this plague as a disaster, was to alter the ecology of the English countryside. Buzzards, finding no rabbits, turned to living on insects and even seagulls that they caught feeding on waste tips. Foxes went onto a far more omnivorous diet. I believe the foxes found scavenging in cities like Birmingham, are the descendants of foxes driven into scavenging by the results of myxomatosis. Stoats, weasels and kin blood did not adapt, however, and became almost extinct.

Just as the ecological face of the country altered, so did the lives of the rabbit catchers. Many warreners just went out of business – for there were no rabbits to trap, snare or shoot. Several gave up their ancient strains of working ferrets, handed down like heirlooms from father to son. Lurchers (whippet or greyhound hybrids) became hard to sell. Just prior to myxomatosis I had friends who lamped rabbits by running these lurchers into a beam of light produced by running a car spotlight off a battery carried on the back of the hunter. Even in 1950, when rabbits fetched less than

64

20p each, I knew men who made a hundred pounds a week simply by poaching rabbits. Not so since myxomatosis. Prior to myxomatosis, I knew two warreners who were ferreting two hundred rabbits a day within a radius of ten miles of Lichfield. Seven days a week they worked and never seemed to reduce the rabbit population. Country town markets were once festooned with rows of gutted rabbits for sale, but this all stopped when the dreaded myxomatosis came. Few rabbits were now offered for sale. Scarcity usually increases the value of the commodity, but not so with the rabbit. A few people complained of having contracted myxomatosis – one even spoke on radio. It was enough to prevent potential customers even looking at a rabbit. No one wanted the rabbit anymore, no longer was he the poor man's substitute for the Sunday roast. Oddly, years later, this attitude still prevails today. One often hears "Since the disease I just couldn't stomach a rabbit at any cost." What utter rot. I have eaten, fed my cats, dogs, ferrets, hawks and eagles on myxied rabbits and have never seen any ill effects. Yet noted poachers will call off his dog rather than let the lurcher come in contact with a myxied rabbit.

Rabbits are fortunately making a comeback. A few days ago I spoke to Alan Bryant of Bryants Rabbit Catching Equipment, and he tells me there has been a boom in the sales of nets, snares, and ferreting equipment. I am now constantly asked to sell young ferrets, whereas before I simply gave them away, and found difficulty finding homes for the hobs which could only be used for rabbiting. Things are looking up for the rabbit and hence for the ferret and ferreter.

When rabbits become numerous again they will start to cause damage and will cease to become a creature to be preserved so that people can pay vast sums of money to shoot them. I believe that the revival of the ferreter and the ferret is on the horizon.

Having now given a brief history of the rabbit, it's on now to hunting him with the ferret. Ferrets should be roughly five months old before taking out rabbiting – you will notice that this is the age when the European polecat becomes independent of his mother. If your ferrets are handled properly as babies, taught that the human hand means good things, not fear and pain, then your ferret will need little training. The wild polecat instinct to explore every nook and cranny is still very strong in the ferret, subsequently few ferrets will refuse to explore the first hole they encounter. Ferrets starting work will always sniff around the edge of the hole before entering it. Be patient. Do not force a ferret down any hole, for ferrets treated like this tend to become very shy at coming out to the human hand. If you have no dog, and I will deal with the training of a marking dog presently, then it is likely that your ferret's explorations of its first earths will be just a little fruitless. The ferret will simply go into the mouth of one hole and come out of another. Don't worry, it is all experience for the ferret and for you. There are many who put a collar and line on a ferret for its first venture into the big, not so wide, world of rabbiting. My advice to anyone doing this is like Mr Punch's on getting married, "Don't". Look at it logically. The line is a decided disadvantage to the beginner's young ferret. If there is nothing in the earth then the ferret will come out anyway. If there is a rabbit underground, then the ferret will try to bolt or kill it. The resulting struggle is going to result in an almighty tangle of the line ferret and rabbit. Furthermore, young inexperienced ferrets rarely flash to the rabbit, but rather explore every nook and cranny underground so that the line is likely to be threaded through every tree root and if one is ferreting a rubbish dump (often good places for rabbits) heaven knows what else will snag the line. It is even money that your ferret will get hung up during his first hunt if you hunt him on a line. The young ferret is unlikely to forget this nasty experience and will develop all sorts of bad faults through it. The result can quite easily be a ruined ferret. The tyro might argue, "but if the ferret won't come out, I can pull him out with the line", and the answer would be, if your ferret refuses to come out he is either hung up or on his prey. Pulling him out is very likely to strangle him. Don't let your young ferret work on the line for the first time out. There is a place for a line ferret and a youngster certainly does not qualify for the title of "line ferret", which I will explain later. Let your ferret work free and come out when he or she has decided the time is right. One piece of positive advice to counteract all the "Don'ts" of the last passage – allow your baby ferret to feed on a rabbit the day before he or she is taken out to hunt them. If you can't manage a whole rabbit, then guts, liver or heads will do. This will give your young ferret greater keenness when she comes in contact with the inhabited rabbit warren. She will know all about the edible properties of the prey she is hunting. Don't listen to cranks who say that a ferret fed this way is liable to go in, kill, and lie up. All ferrets unless muzzled or defanged (a horrid practice), will kill below ground if given a chance. A

66

ferret is not a Springer spaniel, hunting to please its master. It is a partly tamed polecat hunting to slake its hunger or blood lust. The successful ferreter should endeavour to harness this lust, not to stifle it.

Eventually, although if you do not have a dog to make the earths, it may take a little time, your ferret will "connect" and find a rabbit underground. Now is the time when you will discover the strengths of your ferret, albeit your own strengths. Firstly, ferreting is the sport of the silent. People who enjoy clumping about shouting, smoking, and bringing noisy children, should not go ferreting, for your ferret has now the task of convincing the rabbit that it is safer to leave the warren and make a dash for it, than it is to stay underground and face a hostile ferret. If the rabbit is aware that the hunter is above ground, the rabbit is likely to be reluctant to bolt, and try to run around the warren to evade the ferret. When it tires of running around the warren, or is cornered in the numerous blind holes that rabbits invariably dig, it cannot bolt. Rabbits must have a fairly high pain tolerance level for some peculiar instinct causes the rabbit to protect its neck when faced with a stoat, ferret or weasel. Most mustelids kill by the neck bite, and so these blind holes have a purpose. The rabbit simply puts its head into the end of the blind hole and hunches its back, filling the hole and thereby prevents the ferret from getting over the back to make the fatal neck bite. Ferrets scratch away frantically at the well fleshed rump of the rabbit and many even eat pieces off the haunches of the rabbit. Rabbits must have some inbuilt mechanism to resist this exquisite pain. Such a position does, however, have the advantage of preventing or slowing up the ferret making a kill and puts the ferret in a very vulnerable position, for a kick from a powerful hind leg of a rabbit can, if it connects, severely injure a ferret. I once had a ferret come out with a very long gash along its side. At first I thought a rat, but on examining the wound, it was too long and jagged to have been inflicted by a bite. It was the result of a very powerful kick from the hind legs of a rabbit. I often have ferrets kicked about in the rough and tumble below ground (for this reason I dislike minute and weedy jills).

When one's ferret comes out of a warren after several minutes, without being able to bolt the rabbit, then examine its claws. You will usually find that they are clogged with rabbit fur. If a line ferret (and I will explain this term later) is put in, you will usually find that although your first ferret has some muzzle blood and considerable fur on its feet it is still quite likely that the rabbit has "blocked", a term used locally for filling up a blind hole, and the ferret has tried to bolt it, given up, and the rabbit is still very much alive – a little mangled, but still alive.

I had further proof of my theory last autumn and winter, for a great number of deciduous and coniferous trees had been planted on the estate locally. The woodman had surrounded the saplings with rabbit proof netting, so perfectly constructed that a rat could not get through, but a multitude of rabbits did. The woodman, a great friend of mine called John Wall, had trapped and snared, but still the rabbits destroyed the sapling trees. We were asked to exterminate the rabbits on the estate. I say exterminate, not thin out or reduce – exterminate. The estate was several thousand acres and we jumped at the chance of hunting it. We ferreted every moment we could and took a huge bag of rabbits, almost like the pre-myxomatosis days, but we had many ferrets come out with masses of matted blood and fur on their feet. We assumed kills below ground, and as the estate was a very thickly wooded area, did not bother to use a line ferret or dig. Still the damage to the new trees continued and the estate owner began to cast doubts about our hunting ability. To ensure we kept the rabbiting rights on the land we decided to lamp it with a lamp and lurcher. I had in training a neat bull terrier/ greyhound/greyhound bitch called Penguin, on account of some odd mannerisms as a puppy, and she was so soft mouthed she never damaged a carcase and retrieved them alive and squealing to hand. She caught many agile, healthy, rabbits with the hind quarters eaten off them, obviously by ferrets. Clearly not every bloody ferret has made a kill.

When ferreting it is possible to ensure your ferret does not kill underground by a variety of methods. Frankly I dislike all these methods and feed my ferrets before taking them hunting. If they kill they merely nibble a piece of the prey. For those who don't want a subterranean kill and the possible problem of digging, then there are various methods of preventing it. Firstly, there are ferret muzzles shaped like dog muzzles and made of string or leather which can be attached to the head of the ferret allowing it to breathe freely, but not bite the rabbit. Now these can be a bit of a problem, as ferrets usually detest wearing them, and if a ferret is muzzled for the first time and inserted into a rabbit hole, he will spend most

Three types of ferret muzzle.

of his time trying to get the muzzle off before settling down to his work. If you muzzle a ferret for heaven's sake let him get used to wearing a muzzle before taking him out hunting and of course, don't ever take him out rat hunting wearing his muzzle. Alan Bryant of Bryants, Surbiton, is an expert on rabbit equipment. He says that four or five years ago, a new type of muzzle was patented which fitted something like a horse's bit. However, few people found this type satisfactory, and so the model went off the market. This is not the only method of muzzling, however. In South Wales when I was a boy, I saw several barbaric methods used to muzzle ferrets. My youth was at the time when the valleys knew great poverty and the life was hard. Hardship and poverty seem to breed a particularly callous type of person. The would be ferreter would get a very thick glove and a very young ferret. He would then obtain a cobbler's awl and heat it to redness in the fire, boring holes through the upper and lower lips of the screaming ferret. The stench of roasting flesh, coupled with the explosion of the anal scent glands of the ferret is a smell I will never forget. I can remember writing the story in my infants' school newsbook (a great source of unpleasant stories to interest teachers) and my teacher straight out of college, had shown the book to the head, who must have thought that she was teaching a child with a psychotic and macabre mentality. Anyway, the cauterised holes never sealed up and it was a simple method for the ferreter to thread twine through the holes of the upper and lower jaws to prevent the ferret from biting the rabbit. It was a common method of muzzling when I was a boy and subsequently was regarded as perhaps only slightly cruel, but to my young mind it was a savage, brutal and pointless exercise for I had a great love of my own ferret and would not have wanted to sever my mental bonds with it by such acts of brutality.

The third method of preventing underground killing, is to snap off the eye teeth of the ferret with a pair of electrician's pliers. Sadistic, stupid, and insane as this must seem, it is still a common practice. Don't do it. Firstly, immediately the enamel of a carnivore's teeth is chipped, decay sets in quite rapidly. A ferret with just the tip of a carnassial tooth chipped soon develops a decayed eye tooth. Snapping off the eye teeth close to the gum is not only a sure way of preventing a ferret killing a rabbit, it is a sure way of ensuring a short life for the ferret. Decay is rapid and an abscess forms and the ferret's mouth is so swollen that it can't eat and it dies. Furthermore, a ferret so treated must for ever after live on a slop diet for its teeth are incapable of tearing meat without those giant carnassial teeth. Don't break off the eye teeth. It is illegal, pointless, cruel and ruins the ferret.

The real reason why no full-time ferreter will muzzle a ferret is a purely practical one, however. Firstly, the warrens of rabbits are rarely occupied by legitimate tenants only. Rats also lodge in them, particularly if the warrens are near a farm building and the winter is fairly mild. A ferret usually needs little by way of using its teeth to convince the rabbit that it must bolt, but a big rat is an equal match for any ferret. Many will stand their ground and fight. It is an equal match – a big buck rat against a ferret, even if the ferret has his formidable eye teeth, but without these eye teeth, or wearing a muzzle, then the ferret does not have a chance. The trouble is that ferrets are often so courageous that they will attempt to fight the rat even though they are muzzled or defanged. The result is obvious. I once saw a muzzled ferret used on an old tip in Birmingham. True there were rabbits aplenty, but such a place was bound to house rats. The jill went in, tail lashing, and two rabbits bolted, followed, after a while, by the jill whose eye and muzzle strap had been split by a rat bite. I disliked muzzles before, but never used one after that.

Another don't is do not rabbit in summer time. Firstly, the earths are invariably covered up by undergrowth and are difficult to net, but more important still, the rabbit will nearly always have babies in the nest which the ferret will always consider nourishing food and stay to eat them – wasting time, spoiling sport, and ruining more profitable winter rabbiting. Most amateur ferret keepers will try a summer hunt and many are the ferrets that I find wandering during summer time as a result of this summer hunting.

No matter how careful one is, however, the ferret will catch the unsuspecting rabbit underground and after a brief struggle, slay it, eat part of the body, and sometimes lie up. If the ferret is well fed before the hunt, this lying up time is much reduced for the ferret will usually nibble a piece of the head and come straight out. You still haven't got your rabbit, however, and this is where the line ferret comes in. If you intend to ferret regularly, then you will need a good line ferret, so let us discuss the tasks and properties of such a ferret. The line ferret should be big and strong – gentle with man, but sour as hell with other ferrets. He should wear a collar in his hutch as well as out hunting, as this gets him used to this piece of equipment. When a line ferret is put to work a piece of twine (thin but strong) should be attached to the collar of the ferret, and the twine should have knots put in every foot along the line. Remember, the line ferret must be gentle with man but mean as hell with his own kind.

The line ferret.

The jill has gone to ground, killed, and is lying up on the rabbit. Now is the time to take out the hob and place the line on his collar. By noting the number of knots disappearing down the hole as the hob streaks towards the kill, one can roughly gauge where to dig to find the dead rabbit. The hob reaches the kill fairly quickly, for he should be fairly hungry before the hunt and the scent of a bloodied rabbit will usually seem irresistible to him. He reaches the kill, and being surly and aggressive, drives off the jill who, (providing there are no other rabbits in the earth), comes out, slightly upset, but unhurt. The hob now begins to feed on the rabbit again at the head which is the part where most ferrets start to dine. Dig to him quickly before he has a chance to glut himself. A hungry hob will stay on the kill until the ferreter digs right up to him. A hob with a full belly will usually leave the kill to investigate the cause of the banging as one digs near to him. If a line ferret had a union then he would surely be able to claim danger money. Many hob ferrets carrying lines meet with sticky and unhappy ends, by tangling their lines in the tree roots which frequently interlace the warren. If one has a great deal of time, then it is possible to locate him, but if one is poaching an area then I'm afraid that the poor beast must be left there to die of thirst or starvation. A nasty death for any beast.

Some time ago I worked as a teacher in a junior school in Thorpe near Rotherham and as I hated the job and the money was poor, I supplemented my living by poaching the rabbits from a keepered estate near Chapeltown. It was an easy job as I had an attractive girl friend who rode pillion on my broken down motor scooter. She acted as a decoy, always chatting to the keeper, who told her tales of catching huge bands of savage poachers. While she listened to these oft repeated tales I madly ferreted the nearby woods for rabbits. One afternoon my jill had had enough. I had worked her too hard and she lay up on the kill. At that time I had a sour old polecat line ferret who hated other ferrets and flashed to the kill. I lined him, let him race into the earth, settle and began to dig like a fiend for my decoy was rapidly losing interest in the gamekeeper's tales. I dug madly, but not very wisely, for after a few minutes I located a line which was not my own. I dug another spadeful on and found shrivelled ferret remains tangled up in a root. He was still wearing his collar. I dug to my hob and rabbit and we rode back to Rotherham in silence. It was a hell of a way for a ferret to die.

My old friend and co-ferreter, Jeff Elwood, had better luck with his liner. Jeff had one of the best liners I have ever seen. He came by him by the merest chance. A young lad had bred a litter of white ferrets and his mother had made him get rid of them. The ferrets were the wildest I have ever seen. I suggested Jeff bought a whip and a chair before trying to handle them. They were in excellent shape, well fed, but as wild as hawks, for the boy had been reluctant to handle them. Jeff paid 50p a piece and I knew he would be in for a bad time with them. For nearly a month Jeff had nasty bites on his hands and then they settled down. Jeff sold four of the five and kept the largest, meanest hob. At the time I thought Jeff was going to match him against football rowdies in gladiatorial contests to the death, for he was as savage as hell. He would not cage with any jill and went berserk when he saw a strange hob even before the breeding season when hobs get touchy with each other. He was a thug, a real bully, ideal for the job of a liner. One day, Jeff was ferreting near Hinckley in a rhododendron wood when his jill killed and lay up. He put in his liner hob who flashed to the kill and drove off the angry, chattering, jill ferret. Jeff dug to the hob. Warrens in rhododendron woods are frequently deep as the roots penetrate to great depths breaking up the bedrock and the rabbits excavate the shattered rock. Jeff dug for an hour, but to his dismay he found the kill was deep inside the crevice of a rock. He tried pulling the line gently to get the hob off the kill, but with no success. The line was quite firmly latched to some piece of rock. He gave the line an even sharper pull and it snapped. Goodbye ferret. With a very sad heart Jeff came home. It is a very saddening thing to know that one has a ferret die through being hung up for it is a nasty lingering death and the hob had served him well. Jeff thought of Cymaging the earth to put an early end to his old friend, but somehow he just couldn't do it. Cymag would have killed the liner instantly, but Jeff had a faint hope of the hob getting out.

A month later Jeff was hunting the same woods during a pigeon shoot. His springer spaniel began dancing around a gorse bush darting in and barking, almost good naturedly. Jeff investigated and found his furious liner, tail fluffed out, spitting but still wearing his collar. He was as fat as a pig, but as wild as a hawk. He was caught by throwing a coat over him and returned to his hutch, spitting vengeance at Jeff and the dog. It took a further three weeks to tame him, but never was there a better liner. He flashed to the kill, attacked any jill or hob on the kill and drove them out. Furthermore, he would not move from the kill as we dug down to him and although he spat at us as we took away his rabbit, he was as eager to go at the next jill that lay up. Even when we caved in above him, covering him with earth, he still angrily guarded his kill and we always had to pull him off the rabbit.

Some hobs, and even large jills will sometimes try to pull the kill out of the earth towards the ferreter. These are real treasures and no one will usually sell one (though most people boast of having one). Why they do this is a puzzle – wild polecats eat their prey in situ, if they kill below ground they eat below ground and the average polecat is scarcely strong enough to carry a fully grown rabbit back to its nest. I have only ever seen three ferrets that always dragged out their kill (I have never owned one) but I have seen hundreds drag the kill away from the ferreter.

Mrs Beeton says, "First catch your hare" – well, let us now decide how to catch our rabbit. We have persuaded him to bolt – now what next? All that now remains is to catch him. This can be done by using guns, dogs or nets.

Firstly, if one has a twelve bore and stations oneself and a friend or so in strategic positions, puts in a ferret, then the chances are your ferret will bolt the rabbit. That is, of course, if one is quiet. Sadly guns, particularly twelve bores, are not particularly quiet, so many rabbits will sometimes duck back in and face the ferret as soon as they hear the first volley of a shot gun. I have seen this happen all too often and the shooting party move off, allowing me the dubious pleasure of having to dig out my ferret. Some rabbits however will bolt readily even though the gun fire above ground resembles the Battle of the Somme. Rabbits are unpredictable creatures.

The next method is, of course, to station a dog, or dogs, at strategic positions and to wait for the rabbits to bolt. Small lurchers are ideal for this job, for rabbits make a short, sharp, dash before making cover. Large lurchers are great for hare, but they take time to get into their stride and are not really suitable for ferreting dogs. Some of the best rabbiting dogs I have ever seen were Irish terrier or Bedlington Terrier whippet hybrids. They have the whippet's speed and the terrier's blind guts to smash into deep and prickly cover after the escaping rabbits. Whippets are usually a bit thin coated for facing really nasty cover. Teach your rabbiting lurcher to mark inhabited holes by allowing him a few easy rabbit kills in the open.

Myxied rabbits are usually easily caught, and soon he will learn to point to holes which are occupied. Discourage him sniffing down these holes or digging, as this informs the rabbit that there is trouble waiting on the surface. He should be broken to ferret and should never interfere with a netted rabbit that is firmly enmeshed, but should one slip the nets he should nail it. Forget trying to buy such a treasure, train your own. No one in his right mind sells a dog which has all these qualities.

One of our local poachers had an excellent whippet lurcher for this job. He was an accidental mating between an ugly, leggy, rough coated Jack Russell I am ashamed to say I bred, and a pedigree show whippet which belonged to a woman who bred and showed whippets. The terrier had bitten through the fence and was caught tied to the in season whippet. The woman threw water over him, had the bitch injected to abort the litter, but still Bonzo was born. He survived the threat of drowning by being the only pup in the litter, and being kept to take away the bitch's milk. I think Jack paid a pound for him and I remarked, as I looked at the horrid specimen that Jack had been robbed. Never did a dog more belie his appearance nor reward a man more than Bonzo did. If Jack had overlooked a hole, Bonzo marked it, and if the rabbit bolted, Bonzo was on it like a shot. He killed with a deft flick and would dive into the deepest gorse to fetch out a rabbit. Although he was a grandson of my noted ratting dog, San, Bonzo just didn't want to know rats. Sometimes rats bolted before the rabbits and skipped through the nets. Bonzo watched them go, even stepping out of the way for them to pass, but any rabbit which bolted was snapped up instantly. Jack said Bonzo only made one mistake. A huge, pregnant doe rat bolted and Bonzo nailed it – it was something of a draw, for the doe savagely bit Bonzo, who dropped the rat and never made another mistake. Several people made Jack mouth watering offers for Bonzo, but Jack always refused – a hard thing, as Jack had a large family and was out of work. Several people brought whippet bitches for Bonzo to serve, so famous was his sagacity, but he never bred anything of any worth. Bonzo was a one-off job, or as Jack said, "When God made him he broke the mould, so he couldn't make a replica." He certainly was a remarkable dog. He was reared with, and drank from the same dish as two jill ferrets and if either strayed too far into cover, Bonzo retrieved it in his mouth and the unharmed ferret did not seem to object. Oddly enough, Bonzo died of Wiels disease or

Undergrowth should be cleared to prevent the net snagging.

leptospirosis, as it is known in dogs. The irony of the matter is that Wiels disease is usually caught from rats.

I make no bones about it. I like nets for taking bolting rabbits, far better than lurchers and guns. Many times have I been shown how to make these purse nets, and have made a ridiculous mess out of my handywork. There are firms which sell patterns for them, but they are so cheap to buy and take so long to make, that a machine made net is obviously a better bet. I recently visited Alan Bryant of Bryants, Surbiton, who has an amazing collection of nets and who finds them very easy to make by hand, but he also agrees that machine made nets are usually better made, and from terms of time/economy, much cheaper. There was a time when I considered that I was as good a man with nets as any man in the country – and then I met Ray Hemming, a man famed for his netting skill here in the Midlands. When I watched this man net a warren, I realised I had much to learn. He was painfully slow and silent to the point of being annoying, but nothing ever seemed to slip through his nets. His fame as a net man is indeed justly earned. Briefly, placing a net is simply driving a peg in a fairly secure place and letting the net encompass the mouth of the earth. The ring of the net is held in place by either tucking it in the earth at the floor of the earth, or holding it in position by a tiny twig. Ray sets his nets so that they are level with the ground on either side of the hole. Moses Smith,

76

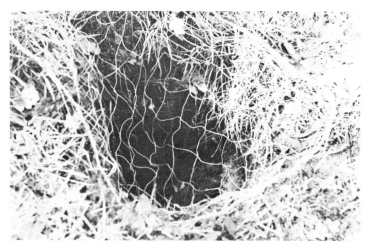
A correctly placed net.

noted gypsy/hunter, usually pushes the net into the earth to give it a slightly concave look. I confess I favour Moses' method, probably because I was taught this method by Tom Evans when I was a kennel boy. Clear away, but quietly, any undergrowth that may snag the net, and thereby preventing the net tightening on the rabbit as it hits the net. Ray's plodding, methodical, nerve racking thoroughness, really does pay off – though I admit it is the cause of my not hunting with Ray as often as I used to, for his slowness at netting used to drive me to a state of frenzy. Gerry, Ray's close friend used to say that Ray's slowness was a matter of economics, for the rabbits in the hole had time to breed three more litters before Ray had the net in position – a slight exaggeration. Yet I never saw a rabbit slip a net set by this slow, plodding, expert, and I must confess I have lost quite a few through rabbits hitting the nets and "throwing" them.

Whyte Melville once said that the best of his pleasure he had with horse and hound. I have a very much more plebian attitude and am perhaps more easily satisfied, but some of the most exciting days I have ever spent have been associated with ferrets. I keep a diary of all my hunts – fifteen rabbits don't become fifty as a result of time if one keeps an accurate diary and certain events stick in my mind. Most tales that are remembered are happy, for one tends to forget bad times and only remember the good – thus, my mind puts an entire screen around my National Service Army days.

One hunt that sticks out in my mind, and indeed the results of that hunt are always remembered when I look in a mirror, occurred in Repton in Derby. At that time I did a lot of rabbiting with Michael Wilkinson, a self taught naturalist, who kept and bred all manner of hawks and foxes etc., in captivity. He hunted rabbits in a stone quarry, bolting them with ferrets and flying them with a goshawk or a type of hawk eagle. He did not have permission to hunt the quarry, for the place was still being worked and I am sure that if Mick had gone there with a gun it would have ensured his instant arrest. Still he used to turn up with his hawk on his fist and when the quarry boss asked his business there, he would reply, "Just training the bird." Mick took no offence at the idiot comment, "What can it say, then," and was left alone as he was probably thought of as one of the harmless inmates of a local institution. He wandered where he pleased with his hawks, and when the laughing, joking, workmen disappeared, down went the ferret and his hawks wreaked absolute murder on the bolting bunnies. In fact they wreaked far too much murder, for he cleared out the quarry. Mick tried to say it was myxomatosis that cleared his pitch, but we all knew better. He had overhunted the place to the point where no rabbit was safe from his feathered killer. The problem was now how to restock the quarry, so that the next year would yield a good haul of rabbits. One day Mick phoned me and said he had found an ideal place. A sheep breeder had just asked a shoot to leave his land as he had had public health reports of number six pellets embedded in the mutton carcases. As he owned pedigree sheep he was against using dogs to hunt, so an idiot with hawk and ferret seemed fairly harmless – after Mick had convinced him that few goshawks could fly off with a sixty pound lamb. (I once lost a trained sparrow hawk and all attacks on sheep locally were attributed to the bird – which weighed ten ounces.) We found the place ideal. Our task was to net all the banks and take out all the live rabbits and restock the quarry. Simple enough, but the plot thickens. I had a tiny polecat jill ferret, a wizard with rabbit and a demon to rat. She was a ferreter's dream, for she would work all day and not lie up once. Neither would she consider working an uninhabited warren. A man could not wish for a better ferret. We netted the first bank on the edge of a farm tip and put in the ferret. A rabbit rapidly exploded from the one hole we had missed, but three large rats obliged us by creeping through

Ferret inserted under the net.

the holes of our nets. After them trundled our angry ferret, who did not suffer fools gladly and we had failed to net her rabbit, or kill her rats. It began to snow, but we were determined to get our rabbits so we tried for the next bank. It was a really deep warren, the result of years of rabbit excavation and was an absolute rabbit fortress that would give a young ferret a nervous breakdown. We put down seventeen nets and blocked minor holes with tightly packed twigs (a good dodge when one runs out of nets). We heard the jill running the rabbits round and round the underground labyrinth and waited in silence. Wham – a doe hit our nets. We unravelled her (quite a task for they kick like mad) and put her straight in the sack where she cowered in the deep hay. We quickly replaced the net and almost immediately another rabbit hit the same net – again unravelled by me – bleeding quite badly from arm scratches. Mike, yet again, replaced the net. Another huge doe chose to hit the nets some fifteen yards away and we raced up and began to free her to put her in the sack. As I did so, up leaped one of the rabbits and hit me straight in the nose. It had been waiting for the sack to open to make its escape. In my agony I dropped the sack and all three rabbits bolted to safety. Mick said something that a longshoreman, or a truck driver, would have considered unpleasant and we travelled back to Repton in silence. Mick can be very violent if upset, and the loss of three rabbits made him decidedly upset. I

Not at home – ferret has not "found" and prepares to leave the warren. Note position of net.

dropped him at home, my nose now swelling up like a man auditioning for a Santa Claus job at a department store. Halfway home I touched my swelling nose and it began to pour with blood, and I mean pour. My shirt, jacket, seats and windscreen, were soon a red, sticky, mess. A crime car passed me and waved me down. I stopped. "Anything wrong, sir?" He added "sir" with just a hint of suspicion. I either had a corpse in my boot, or I had just been on the losing end of an axe duel. "No, officer, a rabbit hit me in my nose," just didn't seem to convince him. He walked around my car a few times, thinking as to whether Moriarty's Criminal Law book covered such an eventuality. He said, thoughtfully, "All right sir, you can go," but followed me back to my house in Lichfield. My nose still bled copiously, so I knew I had broken a bone. I went to Lichfield Casualty hospital for treatment. Here my embarrassment at explaining my accident was to begin again. The Indian doctor gave me a curious enigmatic, oriental glance and wrote something on a piece of paper. I was convinced it was an order for a straitjacket, and prepared myself for a dash for the door, but he merely staunched the bleeding, though from time to time he shook his head, murmuring, "A rabbit, a rabbit." Ernie Phillips' son was once knocked out by a rabbit bolting from a hole and hitting him in the face. It left such a huge bruise that an NSPCC official called on Ernie one night. They left him in peace, but he could tell they did not believe his story. Rabbits bolt with terrific force when pursued by a ferret.

On 28th December 1975, I wrote in my diary the proud comment, "I have never lost a ferret while hunting." Oh, foolish man to tempt the powers of fate. As I finished my note the phone rang. Peter Bates, a sporting Bedfordshire farmer, invited me down for a day's ferreting. "Bring guns, net, dogs, the lot," he said, "we are overrun." Now, I was never classed as a Daniel Boone with a gun, and my army training did nothing to help my marksmanship, but I am a good net man. However, on my teaching staff was a man called John Baker – a male edition of Annie Oakley, who was a phenomenal shot with an air rifle and had just bought quite an expensive shot gun. So we set off for Bedford. Baker commented on his shot gun, "Never used it before," but I was not worried as we had nets aplenty and a brilliant sandy jill, a demon on rabbit, but who would flash out of a warren if a rat was present and refuse to re-enter under any circumstances. She had been badly bitten by a rat during her youth, and just didn't want a re-match with one, but on rabbits she was great. However, just now and again one gets "just one of those days". Rabbits bolted from undetected holes. Baker shot and missed badly, sometimes blaming himself, and sometimes the shotgun. We reached a likely spot. Several runs led into well used holes. I put in my sandy jill, waited a moment, and the thumping began. Baker slipped the safety catch and just waited. A rabbit shot out just under my feet. Baker fired, and missed it, but some shot raked its fur. It didn't want to try for the second barrel, so it flashed into a nearby hole not ten feet from where it had bolted – out flashed my ferret and, before I could pick it up, it had followed the rabbit to ground. Now rabbits, or rats, rarely bolt twice to a ferret and this one was also injured, so my ferret, now tired by a day's work, was in for a field day. It was getting dusk. Hail fell heavily. Baker and I lamped the hole until my battery had run down. Soaking wet, we set out for home with a sad heart, for the loss of such a ferret is an awful blow. We spoke little on the way home. That night I put a line through my comment "I have never lost a ferret". Holidays ended and I returned to school. On the Monday, Baker and I met in the staff room, still saddened by my loss of the ferret. We seemed equally depressed, John apologising and saying it was his fault, and my knowing that I should have been quicker picking up the ferret. It was ten past three and my free period. The phone went, it was

Peter Bates, "Your bloody ferret is running around my pig sty," he said. I confess I played truant and raced to Bedford and was home with my jill before six o'clock. "I have never lost a ferret while out hunting."

Yet I have had several ferrets killed while out hunting. In 1970, I met a falconer who had a large female goshawk. He had obtained her as an adult – a wild caught bird is called a haggard – from Finland. She was an evil beast and would foot my hand if she had half a chance, but she was deadly on rabbit. I've trained goshawks myself, and I know they can be as deadly as a lurcher on rabbit. The French called the goshawk *cuisinier*, hunter for the kitchen, for there is little this valiant bird will not try for when in condition. Goshawks fly rabbit best when in "Yarak" – a Turkish term meaning famished, but still strong enough to take and hold a rabbit or even a hare. I went hunting with this falconer and took with me a yearling white hob ferret – not an experienced hob, but good enough to bolt rabbits for a hawk. Now came the crunch – to convince the goshawk the ferret was its friend and ally, not a creature to be footed and slain by those giant talons. This was done by the falconer jerking the jesses every time the hawk made a lunge at the hob, and shouting "Ware ferret", curiously dated parlance that most of my hunting friends would have replaced with "Give over, you swine," or such like. We found a bank, put in the hob, and a few seconds later the rabbit burst out of the hole. The goshawk slipped – rabbit footed – falconer in with the knife – a matter of a few seconds. Sequel not so funny. Ferret out – goshawk free – ferret footed and ferret quite dead. I accepted our austringer's (a man who trains hawks) apology and we went our respective ways. I think about a year later I was reading his game book and saw entered for the day's "sport" one rabbit and one hob ferret (white). I was angered by this and added as a postscript "death has brightened an otherwise dull afternoon" – and left his house.

I take the death of a good ferret very much to heart, but Alf Jackson, a Midlands shooting man took the loss of his one and only hob ferret a lot more seriously. Alf was a ferret phobe – a man with a mortal dread of ferrets. Out hunting he would jump a mile if one emerged near him. To him they were as they are to the rest of the public – "horrid sods that bite". His friend, Jeff, had a litter of polecat ferrets which his small son, aged four, played with like kittens. Jeff and I were surprised when we noticed Alf appreciating them. One hob stood out in the litter, his coat had the gloss of a starling's wing and he pulsated with playfulness and vitality. He fascinated Alf, so Jeff gave it to him. He was really too young to leave Mum, but Alf said that a young ferret had young teeth, so he took him. He never bit and became the tamest, most tractable hob I've ever seen. He would play with Alf's springer spaniel, retrieve a ball of wool, and allow Alf's daughter to dress him up in her doll's costumes. We took him out at seven months old and to say the least, he was absolutely useless. He went into a hole, ran around, and came out to investigate if Alf was still there, and on finding Alf still there he danced around and tried to make Alf pick him up. I suggested that he needed to see a kill, but Jeff suggested a visit to the furriers, for the glorious pelt would have fetched five pounds. The big hob finished the day with the title of Dopey. We took him out, I imagine, about eight times before it paid any attention to rabbit scent. Then, one day, the penny dropped. He grabbed a young rabbit in a short run-through warren and held him until Alf pulled him out, still gripping his rabbit. From then on it was a home run. Dopey would kill a rabbit and drag it out for Alf to see. When most people want a ferret out of an earth quickly, they simply disembowel a dead rabbit. Dopey came off any rabbit on Alf's call. More incredible still, he would work cover like a rather slow springer spaniel and bolted many rabbits sitting out. Also, when a rabbit bolted from a warren, Alf fired a gun and Dopey raced out to see if Alf had scored a hit. From fool to priceless possession, all in four months. One day, in Alrewas, Alf hunted a pile of mangolas with him. He chased the rabbits over the pile but they refused to bolt, preferring to play hide and seek among the roots. Alf couldn't find him, no matter how he called, and went back next day for him. A gun man greeted him at the gate, "I've just shot a hell of a big sod of a stoat or something," he said (Dopey had seen the man and come out to play). "The sod was going to attack me." Yes, Dopey lay dead among the thistles. He had assumed every man to be his friend and had paid for his error. Jeff said Alf burst into tears, and I never asked him about Dopey, but just afterwards Alf sold his gun and his nets. Jeff and I offered him identically bred ferrets, but sometimes a man forms a link with a beast that, once it is broken, cannot be formed with another. Such was the case with Alf.

On a more happy note (or is it?), the story of my old friend Mark Wibley, who died just a year ago, and there must be considerable laughter in paradise, for no greater comedian ever lived. Ernie considered sending a wreath with a card depicting angels buying a fat man a round of drinks. Mark would have laughed, but I stopped Ernie as it was in bad taste. Mark had a huge hob, far too big for general work, and far too amiable for a liner. He went to ground, killed his rabbit, lay up and we dug. I hated taking the beast out. One day the hungry hob hit a rabbit, two thumps, a squeal, and it was all over. Now, Mark had an odd habit of explaining everything he did as he was doing it. He began by making a squealing, sucking, sound (most ferrets react to this) "I don't believe the ferret thinks the sound the cry of an injured rabbit," said Mark, (Ernie said it sounded like a distressed gnu) "but the ferret merely comes to investigate the curious sound." "They are bright creatures," said Mark, and began to embark on a lecture on intelligence in carnivorous animals. He gave yet another sucking sound, "like a zebra giving birth," said Ernie. "They are," but he did not finish his sentence, for the ferret flashed out of the hole which was filled with Mark's head and latched on to Mark's nose. Mark emerged from the earth with a ferret gripping his nose, and finding it very difficult to look dignified. With quiet aplomb, just laced with fear, he said quietly, "Get it off, Ernie." Ernie eyed the situation and replied laconically, "How?" I squeezed the tail. – A cry of pain from Mark. "He's tightening his grip." I squeezed its paw and again an agonised grunt from Mark – all dignity now gone – "it's gripping harder than ever." Ernie suggested that we took Mark to Lichfield Casualty Hospital, but the thought of sitting in a waiting room with a ferret hanging from one's nose, just didn't appeal to Mark. I finally viewed the immense amount of blood Mark's huge frame was losing and decided that if he moved the ferret's body slightly the blood would run down the ferret's nostrils and choke it. Mark thought the idea macabre, but considerably better than Ernie's idea, which was to cut away part of Mark's nostril with a pen knife. Curiously, my idea worked and the ferret released its death-like grip.

One day in Peterborough I saw a quite amazing sight. I put nets on some holes on a small bank. The dog had marked the earth so there was a rabbit at home. I put in a hob ferret – quite a large polecat hob to be exact. There was a crash and a thump and the ferret came out backwards with his tail like a bottle brush. I put him in again, but he was reluctant to go and turned and came out. I then put in a really sharp, tiny, jill. There was another crash –

another thump, and out came the jill. I looked up the hole and saw a large black rabbit literally attacking the ferrets, driving them out of the warren. This reminded me of a time when I helped out delivering groceries in a place called Wath On Dearne in Yorkshire. A seedy character in a flat cap, sensing the sporting instinct in me, said "Want to see a rabbit thrash a ferret?" My grocery round was going well, and I thought this man was the village idiot who always seems to sort me out as soon as I get to a new district. My curiosity got the better of me and he went around the back of a seedy row of terraced houses and borrowed a good quality white jill – as nice a shape as one could want and as keen as mustard. He put her on the floor of his backyard and loosed out a large chinchilla doe. She fled at the ferret and knocked it over. The jill rolled clear and tried to retaliate. Again the enraged rabbit attacked it, kicking and biting her adversary madly. At last the panting rabbit stood back and the ferret sniffed a dustbin as if to pretend the incident had not taken place. (I lost my job as a grocery delivery man through this incident, which was just as well as I could not reverse the grocery truck.) Tame rabbits have little fear of ferrets and who knows, my Peterborough gladiator might have been a feral rabbit. It is a curious fact, this lack of fear of ferrets in tame rabbits. Has the rabbit lost its innate fear through centuries of captivity, or could the much out of favour Haagerdoorn be right that the tame rabbit is a hybrid between a rabbit and a hare, and through this hare ancestry the fear of subterranean predators has been lost?

A matter of four years ago, Jim French, then terrier man for the Hampshire Hunt, visited my cottage at midnight (Jim's usual visiting hours when he comes north) and brought with him a device for finding lost terriers underground. Jim once did a lot of badger work (a dirty word since the 1973 Badger Act) and had many slogging hours digging for lost terriers. Jim did not really mind as he is a human cyclone with the spade. The device consisted of a receiver and a collar which carried some sort of homing device. He turned on the receiver and the bleeping noise became stronger every time he neared the collar. We tested it, with success, through my massive stone fireplace, and it worked very well indeed. It was, in fact, a ferret locator which Jim had adapted to fit his terrier's collar. Jim swore by this strange device, but Eric Chance had less luck. He dug for four hours through thick clay conglomerate to get to the bleeping. Eventually he located the bleeper and the collar, but the dog was missing as he had cast off his collar and was now fifteen yards in at a badger. Bleepers, or to give them their proper name or title, ferret locating kits, are very useful devices if fitted properly. I have no complaints about the ones I have bought and I have even located ferrets who have killed rats in four feet of hardcore under three inches of concrete. I must decline to say where the incident took place as we were poaching the land at the time – we could have quite simply been arrested for trespass, but we were reluctant to lose the ferret and bleeper. At that time I had some tough, handy, friends with me. Needless to say, we dug, and we didn't do the concrete yard much good in our excavations. A few days later, Ernie brought a local paper which said that a huge hole had appeared in ———— yard and was still unexplained and the police were still investigating the amazing damage. One of my police friends had an explanation for the damage (though the children in my class were in favour of a landing of a Martian rocket). My police friend believed that a fairly substantial robbery had taken place a few years previously and the loot had been stashed in the hardcore before the concrete had been added. I tried to look interested, but my embarrassed face must have given me away. I still visit the yard whenever I go "up north".

I have seen adaptations of the bleeper. One day I went hunting with Henry Clamp, our local doctor, and a great ferreter. We went to Bridgnorth to rid an estate of a great quantity of rabbits that were causing havoc on the sprouting barley. When I arrived I met Jack Legge, a hilarious and inventive character who was the happiest person I ever met. After a fruitless day in pouring rain with a ferret lying up under rock, Jack would rub his hands and say, "Bostin day that – really enjoyed it." At first I thought he was sarcastic, but he really was telling the truth. Jack had made his own bleeper – he works for an electrical firm – from an ancient radio receiver. It was bulky, ugly, but effective, but though it worked well it still picked up stray radio programmes and it was amusing to hear the ferret locating signal coming through Jimmy Young's recipes for fruit pies. Still, I have had some good days with Jack's amusing Heath Robinson devices.

I have already mentioned that I dislike mating close relations together in livestock. If one is successful at this process it is called line breeding, if one is unsuccessful it is called inbreeding. One of the problems of keeping a family of ferrets is that sooner or later inbreeding will throw up a variety of undesirable factors, though it does accentuate desirable factors as well. We keep a family simply because they are very tame (John Abbot, Thuxton, Norfolk also keeps a family because they are very tame and easily handled) and give a reasonable life at rat before quitting – then we put them to rabbits. We have, however, just begun to throw up some undesirable qualities, such as crooked tails and short tails. While such peculiarities are not detrimental to the working qualities of the ferret, it is the warning sign that worse things are to follow, so as soon as oddities appear, try to get new blood. Through inbreeding John Benton, of Redditch, has produced a very tiny strain of ferret, priceless at rabbit and good at rat. He too seeks new blood as he has problems with sterility as a result of inbreeding. One curious quality inherited by just one family I have found very useful. A granddaughter of my favourite old jill, obtained from Ray Hemming, is a medium sized sandy jill, who will not look at a rat, having had early experience of their biting powers. She will trundle a rabbit to the mouth of the earth, untouched, but as soon as it tries to bolt she will seize it by the haunches. At first I thought this a mere coincidence and being trained as a scientist I tend to reject "one swallow summers" as not being the norm. Soon two scientist friends of mine noticed this characteristic and as I had deliberately not mentioned it I decided that it was this jill's particular mode of catching rabbits. We used to put a handful of sticks in a hole to merely delay the exit of the rabbit, and always found the jill clutching a rabbit in the mouth of the earth. I was curious about this peculiar quality so I mated her to her brother – a big, white, line ferret, big enough to hold a bear, let alone a rabbit. One of her young, again a sandy jill, displays exactly the same instincts. However, the litter yielded some very runty little ferrets and I was about to destroy them when Roland Edmonds, a teacher friend and amateur keeper, asked me for the very undersized sister of the sandy youngster, another sandy, but not much bigger than a very large mouse. Not only was she tiny, but she had a hideously twisted, truncated tail (next generation an outcross for our strain). He invited us to Hereford to watch his mini ferret work, for we had teased him dreadfully about it. Roland netted all visible holes and put in the micro ferret. Sure as dammit, a rabbit exploded through an insecure net and flashed across the field. We all muttered, "Well done, Roly," as a means of showing our approval of his netting skill. The big doe shot across the field and came to an abrupt halt and keeled over. I had no doubt she had hit a snare placed with deadly accuracy along her run, and three times as lethal as a snare in a hedgerow. I raced over to investigate and found Roly's tiny ferret with her teeth sunk into the rabbit's brain. I believe she had inherited her mother's peculiar tendency to hold at the mouth of an earth and lacked the weight to do the job effectively. I have several times watched jills ride a rabbit across a field, but are usually shaken off by the bucking of the rabbit.

Having first caught your rabbit, what will you do with it? Pardon the pun, Mrs Beeton. If you catch only one or two, these are usually eaten by the family. If you are a keeper or an estate warrener, then the estate owner will probably know a game shop that will take a large number of rabbits. When I first came to this area I was desperate for money to buy the tiny cottage I now own. I poached every conceivable place merely to stay alive. The numbers I caught were enough to keep me in meat for a year or so until I became more prosperous (I still have long ears, so my friends tell me), but also to pay off the mortgage on my then dreadful shack of a cottage. I found regular sales for a few among the village folk and I avoided the gameshops like the plague, as they were likely to ask where I had obtained these rabbits and I knew the police would be more than interested as to the whereabouts of my sources. Many of the older inhabitants of the village would buy rabbits from us, but the new dwellers who had come to the village to travel each day to work in Birmingham would not consider them. They still had horrid dreads of contracting some human form of myxomatosis and arriving at the office looking like a Quatermass victim. Most of my clients wanted the rabbits skinned, which suited me fine as I dried and sold the pelts in Ashby – a wild rabbit skin will fetch a better price than the skin of a tame rabbit as these skins are used for felt making and the urine and dirt of the warren makes the wild rabbit pelt more suitable for felt than the skin of hutch reared rabbits. I sold numerous rabbits to an elderly Polish couple who had survived the last war in a concentration camp in Germany. They never would take a ready skinned rabbit as I believe they had a horror of being sold a cat as a substitute for a rabbit – they had been forced to eat many cats during the war years, they told me. We had another regular buyer in the form of a German biologist, now retired, but a fascinating wealth of animal lore. He wanted his rabbits skinned, but the kidneys left in. Ernie said that the Germans used the kidneys to make some form of paté, but I knew better. The kidneys of a rabbit are like the kidneys of a man, the left is higher than the right. In a cat they are level. My German too distrusted us to the point where he considered we would substitute a cat for a rabbit.

Every ferreter who hunts rabbits (and even rats) will have seedy offers for live rabbits from the dog racing fraternity, for live rabbits to train track greyhounds. For my sins I have helped to spread myxomatosis, but I have never supplied live rabbits to train a track dog. I am a hunter, not a baiter of wild animals and the thought of a wild animal like a rabbit, cowering in a sack waiting to be turned loose on a track to encourage a dog for its next money making race, brings about instant nausea in me. The antiblood sport people would do well to neglect the artisan hunter with his ferrets, terriers and lurchers, and seek out information on the methods used by callous brutes to train their dogs to run on unlicensed tracks. My rabbits are killed quickly and painlessly.

8 Ratting

I was born in a mining valley in South Wales. Once it was a beautiful valley where a squirrel could jump from tree to tree without touching the ground from the Carn mountain to the edge at Tondu at the lower end of the valley, but by the time I was born the fair country had long been raped, and the place was a wilderness of slag heaps and spoil piles which smouldered evil fumes as the pyrites burned by spontaneous combustion. It was not a pretty place by any standard and rabbits were a seldom-seen novelty, for no self respecting bunny would be seen dead in such a district, but along the bottom of my valley ran a filthy, polluted brook which fed the coal washeries and along the brook lived the most fascinating of all sporting animals – the rat.

Rats abounded in the brooks on the floors of the valley and, together with a crowd of rowdies I had palled up with, I spent my spare time hunting these rats with terriers and ferrets. When the water was low, we had a good haul and I played truant from school regularly during these times. My parents were aware of my interests, and turned a blind eye to them, hoping these interests would pass and I would forsake my good for nothing friends and join a youth club, or attain the zenith of our rather insular society – the Pontycymmer tennis club. When I dropped two of my rowdy friends and joined the Ffaldan Working Men's Library they were overjoyed, for they had visions of my bringing copies of Milton, Chaucer, Keats and other greats. However, when one day they found a pamphlet called "The Mating Habits of Rodents" and a book called "Mice and Rats As The Enemies of Man" in my bedroom, they finally panicked, and took me to a doctor about my unwholesome interests. He said they were a result of teenage fantasy/curiosity and I would soon grow out of it and that, with luck, I might even make the tennis club. He told my mother to forget her worries about my interest in rats, as I would outgrow these morbid interests. Of course I didn't. The rat became a consuming passion for me.

90

Poor old Mam, she died still wishing I had made the committee of the tennis club. If only she had lived long enough to realise that I was to become a biologist, not a rat catcher.

Just as Christianity thrived under the savage persecution of early Roman Emperors, so did my interest in rats thrive under the ever watchful eye of my mother, whose ambition was to see my interests rodent free. At fourteen I entered a Natural History Quiz on British Mammals and, as all my questions seemed to be on rodents, I won quite easily. My parents took a new look at me as I clasped my prize "British Wild Animals", and my mother, with the look of someone who had now finally accepted that her son was a were-wolf, or vampire, said "I suppose if he is happy being a rat catcher, then that is what counts." Rat catcher! Nothing was further from my mind. I wanted terriers and ferrets to hunt the creatures, not to poison them and find their smashed bodies in my traps each morning. By now, however, I had begun my serious study of rats and it was to be a study that helped me take some of the largest hauls of rats recorded in Britain. To hunt the rat successfully you must first learn his habits and weaknesses. James Adams, the philosopher hunter, once said "At first I studied the grisly in order to hunt him. Now I hunt him in order to study him." So was it to be with me.

For a brief spell two species of rat existed side by side in Britain – the black rat and the brown rat. Neither, however, were natives of Britain. In 984 Pope Urban decided that a crusade was necessary to stop the internal strifes of Europe and launched a war against the Moslems of the Middle East. The returning crusading ships brought back spices, silks, the spoils of the Turks and – the black rat. It was a smaller rat than the rats we see today, weighing only about eight ounces. As it was a tree dweller in its native orient, it found that the thatched cottages of England and Europe pleased it greatly. It certainly bred at an alarming rate, though not with the fecundity of the brown rat, and soon no village in Europe was without the black rat. In Germany the legend of the pied piper, which contains more than a grain of truth, showed the dreadful problems it caused. Few poisons were known that could harm these rodents. They were a little too fast and arboreal for dogs to do much damage to them, and it was pointless to ferret them as they simply skipped from rafter to rafter, evading the less nimble ferret.

Europe at that time was the ideal breeding ground for the rat. Sewage was tipped into the gutters of the street, and waste from houses cluttered the roads. People from more genteel areas avoided these slums, but when they were forced to come to these districts, always carried bunches of violets to keep away the "vile vapours" of the city streets. Pigs roamed everywhere and fought with dogs and rats for the household waste and human faeces that cluttered the gutters. I suppose in some ways the rat did much to reduce the city stench as it ate up the garbage and filth, reducing it to innocuous looking, but deadly, rat pellets, which, though riddled with salmonella, typhus, plague and God knows what, did tend to neaten the city streets. In Italy, one Italian doctor put forward the notion that the rat was a useful, unpaid, dustbin man, and actually recommended that people encouraged the rodent in the cities. It was not until the Royal Society was formed that people began to realise that the animal was responsible for the great population controller of the Middle Ages, namely the Black Death. The fleas which inhabited the rat were also partial to human blood, and thus the disease was transferred from rat to man and vice versa – the result, a massive death rate for the flea carried disease – the Bubonic Plague, or Black Death. Europe reeled under the repeated outbreaks of this killing disease, and soon began to clean up its cities. By the eighteenth century man's sanitary habits had begun to change. Pigs were forbidden by law to grub about in the streets – proper drains were constructed and the rat population began to dwindle. A curious fact about the Black Death, was that the Romans had a shrewd idea about its cause, for in the temple of the plague god, two statues of golden black rats were to be found. The ancients realised that an increase in these rats meant high incidence of the plague – a wisdom to be forgotten until the seventeenth century. Anyway, by 1700 *rattus rattus* – the black rat, was well on its way to extinction. Its departure was further hastened however by the arrival of his Asiatic cousin.

The brown rat, *rattus norvegicus*, arrived in Britain about 1760. At first it was called the Norwegian rat – no one knows why, and the name stuck – *rattus norvegicus* – the Norwegian rat. It did not however come from Norway. Just before the beginning of the 1700's the brown rat was confined to an area along the Caspian sea living on seeds and suchlike. It is my belief that after that date a more savage mutation appeared, more carnivorous, more aggressive and more vigorous. It just had to oust its seed eating brethren and soon the native land was overpopulated with this new variety of rodent. Certainly brown rats were arriving in Europe before 1760 and by 1763 naturalists were noting its presence in Britain.

The black rat, now toppling on the rim of extinction in Britain, was pushed well over the brink by the new rival who was bigger, stronger and could outfight him, and certainly outbreed him. Poor old *rattus rattus* didn't have a chance. His brown cousin had ousted him from the rapidly shrinking street middens of the 18th century and the new interest in public health finally saw off the black rat. True he could climb like the squirrel, for he was by nature a tree dweller, but thatched roofs were being replaced by the uglier and cheaper slate and tile, so even his nesting places were disappearing. Sans food, sans shelter, sans public approval, he could do little else but do the honourable thing and become extinct. He now exists as very much of an unsavoury rarity, eking out his last days in the Port of London – more of a relic of the past, not so Merrie England, than the pest he was once considered.

Rattus Norvegicus was here to stay, however. He had all the qualities to survive in a world already hostile to rats. He found England, and the English countryside, very much to his liking, as he found the rest of the world, for few places, other than water free deserts or polar ice caps, are devoid of rats. Originally he was a seed eater, munching grains in his native Asia – now he had readily adapted to take any food so unpalatable that even his black cousin might have refused it. Anything remotely edible is considered fair game and is eaten. Like Jack London's legendary Buck in "Call of the Wild", his body is able to extract vitamins from compounds which were hitherto thought vitamin free. In the 1930s when man, preparing for an international conflict, suddenly took an interest in vitamins, he used as his experimental victim the domesticated *rattus norvegicus*. He kept him on vitamin free diets and the rat resorted to tail eating, filth eating and cannibalism, but survived. Rats will live on food in such a state of putrefaction that even a vulture will die of ptomaine poisoning. Without man's poisons, gassing and ferreting he would become a brown skinned juggernaut, ready to roll flat the world. People may hate him, fear him, and kill him, but only a damned fool could not respect his great tenacity and zest for life.

Just as the black rat donated free of charge the Black Death to human beings, so the brown rat is equally generous with an even deadlier, though not nearly as infectious bug – Wiels disease. In the early days of rat catching, where catchers killed off few by poisons, but more by traps and ferrets, they were paid tail or head money for every rodent they could produce, but a more profitable game was to provide thousands of live rodents for the savage entertainment of rat pits, where rats were tipped into a pit and a dog, usually of bull and terrier ancestry, was given a chance to show how many he could slay in a set time. Billy, a noted bull and terrier hybrid, killed 1,000 in fifty-four minutes. The profit made by the rat catcher in providing this flood of rats for almost nightly performances, was great, but so were the risks involved. There came a time when there were fewer rat catchers prepared to hand catch and provide rats for these rat pits, for many had died of the mysterious rat catcher's yellows – a disease which resembled ordinary jaundice, but which defied treatment and made the rat catcher an emaciated yellow corpse in, perhaps, a week. All mammals can contract this disease from rats, though my ferrets are fed them and seem curiously resistant to the infection. Monlux, a noted scientist, realised the need for research on this malady and came back with alarmingly frightening statistics. Roughly fifty-five percent of all healthy rats were capable of transmitting this disease. Putting it in layman's terms, the odds are that one in every two rats caught by you has this infection and is capable of infecting you, your dogs and God knows what on your premises.

Brown rats breed at a great rate. If the temperature is right, and it invariably is, for rats have bred in the deep freezers of ships bringing meat from foreign parts, they are very prolific. Rats are born naked but soon sprout a coat of thin grey fur. At five weeks old a rat loses its baby coat and becomes brown, this is a sign that puberty has begun and both bucks and does are fertile. Few adult rats will attack a grey youngster for its colouration indicates immaturity and poses no threat to the dominance of an adult buck. As soon as a buck loses his grey coat he becomes a threat to his fellow bucks, and savage battles ensue – a rat fight is really worth watching. I have watched many as I have sat in silence on Mexborough tip. So savage is the conflict that I marvel at the ferret valiant enough to tackle these ferocious and furious rodents. A buck rat savagely defends his territory against all male members of his species. He will allow no intrusions from foreign buck rats whom he considers as a threat. At one time I ferreted a filthy brook in Yorkshire. When a rat, bolted by ferrets, was missed by my terriers, he swam the shallow brook and if pursued by them, took refuge in the bank opposite. The brook probably constituted a boundary, and the rats on the other side of the brook regarded him as an antagonist. He would flash into a hole in the opposite bank, but we would station our terriers around the hole in absolute confidence, for we knew that the other rats would drive out the intruder with more hatred and venom than would any ferret. Even my terriers began to learn this lesson in biological territory guarding. Once, when waiting for the invading rat to be driven out of its territory, I trapped an adult, pregnant, doe under my foot, and took her alive by hand. She had bolted straight away to the ferret, so he had not marked her, but the rats on the far bank had savagely mauled the doe when she had sought refuge in an alien colony. Again praise the courage of a ferret who will venture into the jaws of death to flush out one of these rodents. It is a point to remember when one considers that the rat is such a terrific fighter when you label your ferret a coward when she jibs rats after about eighteen months of steady ratting. A stoat is roughly the same size as a jill ferret and has about the same fighting ability, (and also six times the speed) but few stoats will consider tackling an adult rat. They may chance a few encounters when the stoat is young, but they soon learn the adult rat is a little too much for them. This, I hope, will help you not to expect too much from your jill ferret.

Have no fear your quarry will become extinct – for there is little fear that an animal with their breeding rate will become uncommon, let alone rare. Their breeding rate is astronomical – at five weeks in warm weather, and with good food – a rat can mate and produce young after a brief twenty one day gestation period. The litter size can be up to sixteen, though eight to twelve seems to be the average. The brown rat is an opportunist, where food is plentiful then big litters appear. As soon as young are born, she mates again – on the same day of parturition and twenty one days later the cycle is repeated. Dr Jan Hanzek believes that only three litters are produced a year, but most rats breed in warm buildings and, as with rabbits, temperature is an all important factor. My own researches, conducted in warm battery houses, suggest that at least eight litters are born a year, for in these conditions young are born all the year round. Rats rarely live for more than a year – one of two years old would be considered a veteran. Age manifests itself with greyness, white faces, and poor teeth. Perhaps this greyness is a way of showing the virile buck that the old rat is not a threat to territory, for old rats get as grey as nestlings.

Right, we have discussed the fighting ability of the opposition – now let us decide how to enter and train our gladiator. At the time when Ike Matthews wrote his ratting book there were people ready to discard the ferret for the mongoose as an animal to hunt rats. The mongoose is tame, and a good killer, but cannot touch the good jill ferret as a hunter. I have seen men use a small type mongoose – not nearly so effective as a ferret. Forget hobs for ratting. They are just too big and frankly too slow. Jeff Elwood once told me a story of a hunt in Alrewas, near Lichfield. He was using a large white hob to ferret a warren. The hob was used often as a liner and sizewise big enough to make mincemeat of a rat. Two rabbits bolted, and Jeff and his brother shot both. After a brief lapse, a big doe rat ambled almost casually out. She was heavy in young in spite of the cold winter, and Jeff shot her. As she rolled over, a red ruin that had once been an attractive white hob, appeared. He was very badly bitten and had also been clawed quite badly along the face. The rat had one small bite on her body. The hob should easily have matched the rat in combat. He was as big as she was and damned well equipped to fight. Jeff was convinced a small agile jill would have had little trouble with this big doe rat.

You will need many jills if you are to hunt rat regularly. After a while, particularly after hard battles, a jill will no longer want to work rat. Don't force her in a hole, she has simply had enough, try another jill. I remember one unhappy occasion when we were ferreting a maggot factory in Yorkshire. These are always havens for rats. We were working a pile of bones whose flesh had been stripped off by maggots many years before. The pile of bones had been covered with a thin layer of soil, probably to try and prevent the horrid smell – which it didn't – and the bone catacombs below provided a great breeding ground for rats. My old jill ferret, Medusa, who still had both her eyes at this time, was hustling the rats around the bones. We were not having much success at bolting them, for not only had they numbers enough to fight, but they had literally cubic metres of bones in which to play hide and seek. We were not the only people who hunted this glorious rodent haven (Tony Capstick described it as Disneyland where Mickey Mouse came out, slashing hell out of your ferret). Another man, about forty or so, and his two sons, were also ferreting the other bank. Their ferret,

96

a large, good quality white jill, had gone in and bolted four or five rats, been badly bitten, and then came out with her nose nearly torn off. She came out tail first and her tail fluffed with fear and anger. Obviously a doe rat had newly born young in the hole and had set about the jill, driving her off and slashing her badly. At first the man tried to coax her back; he seemed to be ill informed as to why she was refusing to go back, but she refused for she knew what was waiting around the bend of the hole. He eventually pushed the jill in, and prevented her exit by placing his foot over the hole. There was a fearful squeaking, and the jill desperately tried to come out. "For Christ's sake, man, have some pity," I said, but his answer did not bear repeating. Tony Heath, who lectured in biology and was another amiable giant, was a little more persuasive, however. A rat had bolted, scared out by Medusa's hounding and Tony had trapped it alive under his hobnailed boot. "Pick it up, man," he coaxed. The man blanched. "You must be bloody mad to think I'd pick up a rat," he said, "it'll bite hell out of me." "A twelve ounce ferret is forced to go in and mix it, but a twelve stone man is afraid," Tony sneered. I think our fellow hunter must have felt just a little ashamed and released his foot. A hellishly mauled albino bloodbath emerged from her hole, both ears bitten off close to the head, one eye completely bitten out, and a hellish wound in her side where the ferret had tried to turn to come out of the hole, but the rat had attacked her side. One of the ferret's ribs had been bitten through, so heaven knows the damage done to the internal organs. I have never seen such a badly bitten ferret and I doubt whether it would survive such a mauling. The ferret undoubtedly died. I have never actually seen a rat kill a ferret, but I have had many die from the subsequent maulings. Enough is enough. When a jill refuses to go to rat she is still useful for rabbits, but they usually do not want to encounter rats again. Some jills, as I have stated, will take ferocious maulings and still go back for more. I had a great grand-daughter of my now one eyed Medusa – as gentle as her ancestor was savage, and as peaceful as she was evil. At that time we ratted every night and she took some dreadful beatings from the rats. Three years later I moved to the Midlands. Again she hunted rats for three more seasons, though not as frequently, for we had left our northern rat Shangri La. Still she took some bad beatings in the Midlands, for the rats are no different from those up north. She was still going strong when one day a young rat tried to bolt. She held it by the hindquarters so it could not. The rat turned and gave her a nip between the eyes. The ferret winced, but held on and I killed the rat. I cleaned the wound – not particularly deep though it had reached the bone, but she refused to eat and drink. Three days later she had died. Her body was capable of taking no more sepsis and the last straw had really broken the ferret's back!

Always clean up rat bites as soon as you can. We use proprietary brands of antiseptic like Milton or Dettol. There is little to be said for the salt and water treatment recommended by gamekeepers, though it may have some cleaning effect. Rat bites suppurate badly if they are untreated. They look dreadful when they become septic, dripping large quantities of pus. Furthermore, the wounds are usually in places where ferrets cannot lick, i.e. the face, the neck and head areas, so the ferret has no chance to use the natural antiseptic qualities of its own saliva to counteract the infection. Curiously, the saliva of carnivorous animals contains very strong antiseptics – remember the story of Lazarus who had his sores licked by dogs. I knew one gamekeeper who swore by using diluted carbolic acid (the earliest man made antiseptic discovered by Joseph Lister). His ferrets healed well but left huge scar tissue patches, for though the flesh healed, the fur was burned badly by the acid.

I believe that the ratting life of a jill can be increased slightly by allowing young ferrets to feed on rats. This certainly makes them much keener. I have also noticed that a jill who has taken a dreadful beating from a rat and quit, will often forget her beating if she is worked on rabbit for a year or so. I found this method, of letting an animal forget, works on most creatures. A terrier that is worked to fox and suffers a bad biting, should be retired to hunt rat for a year. He will usually forget the bad times with a fox and re-enter. A snag here however, and it is an obvious one: rats frequently inhabit rabbit warrens.

The ferret keeper will probably find it quite difficult to obtain rabbiting country without paying a good price for it – and shoots which only harbour the humble rabbit fetch a good price these days. The rabbit is now a very shootable commodity. He will have little difficulty in obtaining ratting places, however. At first farmers looked a little askance when I turned up with two terriers and a bag of ferrets, and asked to do a spot of ratting. "No rats 'ere," was always the comment, for few farmers will admit to having any rats on their premises. After a while it became known that my ferrets don't savage anyone, my terriers were not stock worriers, and that in spite of my unkempt appearance, I did not steal scrap iron, lead and copper, and I was frequently invited to do a spot of ratting. Poultry farms were great places, but you will need a large team of men to help ferret a poultry farm or battery house, as if your ferret comes out unnoticed, the ferret will find poultry far more attractive than rat (remember the origin of the word polecat). If you are not quick at picking up your ferret, then there is usually a pile of dead birds to pay for. Maggot factories are, as I have stated, absolute havens for rats – but are such filthy places that the bitten ferrets always fester. Furthermore maggot factories stink, and that is an understatement. Any animal that dies of something unpleasant, rotting fish, offal, tripe that is just a little rank, and even dogs and cats finished up as maggot food. If you can ever get the ratting rights on these places, jump at the chance. You will never ever be short of rats. I regretted leaving the North with its piggeries, maggot factories, and poultry houses and when I came to the Midlands it took me months to get ratting pitches as good as I had left.

When acquiring a rat "pitch" you would do well to take the owner's stories of rats with a pinch of salt – say a bar or so. "We are overrun with rats" usually means "we've seen a rat in a barn." They're the size of cats, usually means they are about average size – say twelve ounces or so, for rats have a way of making people exaggerate. We were only once given an accurate account of the rat population of a district. We used to collect poultry offal to feed to dogs, ferrets, cats and what have you, and the woman who owned the place always begged us to come ratting. "We are literally overrun," she would say, "there are droves of them." For weeks something happened that prevented us taking up her offer of giving us a night's ratting. I would either be lecturing or out hunting, and she eventually said that she would have to order a quarter of a ton of poison if we didn't come. A quarter of a ton set us thinking – if one rat eats two ounces in – but we forget the junior school arithmetic and went. "Hells bells," said Jeff. The place was alive with the biggest rats I have ever seen. We spent every day there, killing well over a hundred a day – they cascaded from troughs, from walls, from doors, as soon as we put in a ferret. Our dogs and hunters had a whale of a time, but not so our ferrets. The rats had been driven in and were reluctant to bolt. Furthermore, there were such a myriad of rats below ground that when we entered two experienced white jills, we heard shrieking and squealing, but although we heard a great deal of running about below ground, few rats bolted. They were playing hide and seek with the ferrets in the hard core below the concrete. We were a bit alarmed at the fact our ferrets had not appeared, for we feared they had gone into another poultry house and destroyed fowl like fury. However, after an hour or so they re-appeared from the same hole as they entered, very badly bitten. We flushed rats from walls easily, but the concrete floor was a death trap to ferrets. The moral of the story is that if you ever get an offer of a rat pitch, no matter how improbable, then investigate it.

Very well, you have found a good place for rats. You are certain they are there. Now comes the time to start your ferrets on rat. Rule one – don't hunt a baby ferret on rat. Wild polecats take roughly five months for the babies to become independent of their mothers. That is the age to try a ferret to rabbit, but remember, a rat is a far more formidable opponent than even my Peterborough rabbit, so the jill needs either some skill at rabbit hunting, or at least to be about seven months old. As I have stated, if possible the jill needs to be fed on rat to get her really keen. Take your jill to the rat hole and let her sniff around the entrance. She will usually creep slowly into the hole, easing in her body like a snake, for rat holes are not usually very wide. Also the ferret is not a stupid creature and will sense the dangerous nature of rats before she has even met a live one. If a rat is present, one of two things will happen. If the rat has young old enough to run about – three weeks or so old, then the colony will bolt, Mamma first. The ferret will usually be able to grab a baby rat as the hindmost bolts. She will have no problem with a baby rat, so the squeaking and squealing usually gives way to crunching as the ferret nibbles the now dead rat. Do not bother to dig her, let her get flushed with triumph with her first kill. She will come out later as soon as the sweet smell of success palls on her. She will need these early successes, for like as not the next hole will house a doe rat with young just a few days old. Does with young this age will defend them against a dog, or even a man. She will certainly not give way to a young ferret. It will be a battle to the death – rat against ferret, for a rat with babies that are helpless will always put up one hell of a fight. The maternal instinct quickly conquers any fear of the ferret. Once in Swinton, Yorkshire,

100

Tony Bell, who owned some excellent working Borders, put a jill ferret to ground in a tip. There was a tremendous rumpus below ground, with squeaking rat and squealing ferret. The rat failed to bolt, so reluctantly Tony took out a scoop of earth with a spade. We found a mother rat covering her two- or three-day old babies, fighting off the ferret. She even attacked the ferreting spade in her efforts to protect her babies. We threw back the earth and left her, taking our ferret to another hole. It would have been a sacrilege to kill such a courageous doe. Jack Ivester Lloyd describes the rat as a coward. How wrong he is. The rat wants no trouble, but if unable to bolt, or if a doe has young, she will fight like a wildcat.

If you merely intend to flush rats from holes, then your problems are over. If you intend to catch one, then your problems are just about to begin. Unless you are as they say locally, "a dab hand with a stick" and can hit any rat as it bolts from the ferret (if you can you should be a star in a Chinese Martial Arts film) for with speed like that you can make a fortune, then you will either need nets or dogs to nab the rat. Now set yourself a Herculean task, try to find a firm that makes rat nets. Alan Bryant boasts he had every type of net, but *not* rat nets. Moses Smith used to ask the wives of his friends for old tights and stockings. At first we thought he had a strange perversion, but he actually used them to make rat nets. The rat nets were made by making a ring of soft, pliable, wire. Moses then stretches the top of the stocking around the ring and pegs them over the rat hole. I have seen many rats caught this way, and in my mining valley home, seen much money bet that no one could take the rat out of the stocking alive. I never saw anyone able to do it, though I saw many a miner with badly bitten hands. Rats caught like this should be killed quickly, not beaten to death. Swing the body against the tree (still in the stocking) or give it a hard blow with a spade. Sometimes two or three rats will dive into the stocking. They never seem to bite their way out – though it would be very easy for them to do so (for a creature whose teeth are sharp enough to eventually get through ferro-concrete.) Moses has had massive success with this method of trapping, but I confess I have not. I have neither his strange skill with metals, nor have I his skill with the needle for his stitching ability resembles a close up scene from General Hospital. I have never been successful with making nets of any kind, therefore I never net rat, but I catch more rats than most.

I use dogs – terriers or small terrier bred lurchers for choice. Ike Matthews suggests that a dog with pointer blood be the choice for the job of nabbing rats. I admit I have never used such a cross and I often wonder as to whether Matthews did. Gun dogs are very soft mouthed, usually, though I once had a cross bred labrador who would kill rats like fury. I think I should go for a working terrier every time. Terriers are bred for the task of killing rats. They have had generations of rat killers bred in them and they are, therefore, just that bit more likely to become a good ratting dog than a chance bought mongrel. A rat can give a dog a really nasty bite. Rawdon Lee, in his ancient book *Terriers* states that he has seen a dog who was the village bully, the terror of all other dogs locally, squeal and run when he finds a rat anchored to its nose. Unlike a rabbiting dog, which is required to catch its game unharmed and undamaged, the rat dog must finish his foe quickly and with a fierce bite or else he will sustain considerable punishment.

If you intend to rat then you need a dog that is agile, fast thinking, and very hard, and your obvious choice is a working terrier, terriers such as Cairns, Scotties and fox terriers will kill rats, but for the regular ratter I suggest he goes for one of the three breeds still shown at working terrier shows (shows not recognised by the Kennel Club). Choose either a Lakeland, a Border, or one of that motley collection

The correct manner of marking a hole – the rabbit is unaware of the dangers above ground.

102

The incorrect way of marking a hole. Dog is down hole scratching at the warren entrance thereby telegraphing his presence to the ferret.

of terriers known collectively as the Jack Russell terrier. Drabble, in his book *Pedigree Unknown* suggest that his best ratting dogs have been Staffordshire Bull Terriers. I have found them slow, clumsy and very immature when they reach seven months old – the age that most terriers are very keen on ratting. They were probably a lot faster when Drabble was a boy, as they had not been influenced by the show bench people and the most famous ratting dogs of the London pits had bull and terrier blood. The show breeders have turned out a heavy massive shouldered dog that looks like a pugilist, but your dog is required to kill rats, not look like the weigh in for the heavyweight championship of the world. Stick to either Borders, Lakelands or Russells.

If you choose a Lakeland, I would avoid the Kennel Club Lakeland, but go for the sort still worked in the fell country; then they are usually keen to kill rats, or for that matter anything, by the time they are six months old. Most Lakelands have reasonable noses and are so hard mouthed as to give excellent value as ratting dogs. Lakelands have a thick coat and therefore will suffer in silence the punishment taken when ratting in hawthorn, gorse or bramble. They are not, however, without problems, particularly if they are worked alongside another dog. John Winch and Cyril Tyson – working Lakeland experts – once visited my cottage to discuss my book on the working terrier. Tyson described the Lakeland as "quick to take offence". What is meant by this terse comment is that Lakelands are bred to be the hardest terriers on earth (or should that read below earth, for they were created to kill fox below ground – kill, not bolt, them). They are, therefore, a fiery bunch and often set about strange dogs that your friends have brought with them. Not only are they a bit short tempered with dogs, but should a rat bolt and be killed by the dog, and the excited ferret emerging after its prey chance to nip the dog (and this often happens), then unless your Lakeland is very well broken to ferret, he will find his fighting blood roused and retaliate – the result is a very dead ferret. Cyril states that constant familiarity between dog and ferret is more than necessary with Lakelands. Still, if one is aware of their quickness at taking offence, then the Lakeland is a superb ratting terrior. Most will take the most vicious bites without complaint and are usually so strong jawed that they will kill a rat at a crunch. I confess I like Lakeland terriers, though I once saw one run amok on some ferrets I owned.

You may wonder what is wrong when you try to start your first Border. Borders are strange dogs for the silly puppy does not grow quietly into adulthood. He remains a puppy for some time; silly, playful and regarding rats as an interesting spectacle to view, rather than tackle; then one day he is an adult, slaying rats like a demon and going to fox and badger with fury. Borders remain puppies for far longer than any other breed of terrier. They are notoriously slow to start work. Many will not look at a rat until they are a year old, so do not be surprised if you find your yearling Border terrier wagging its tail as if to greet a rat as a long lost friend. Sooner or later they will start work and will be nailers to rat. Furthermore, they are so phlegmatic that they are most unlikely to retaliate when an angry ferret nips them. There is much to commend the Border. I believe they are the most intelligent of terriers and providing one makes allowance for the fact that they are slow

104

starters, then you will find the border an ideal ratting dog. I once trained "reject" Borders as part of my living – by reject I mean other people had not been prepared to wait until they had matured, or had partly ruined them by early entering – and have never seen one of these terriers nip a ferret even when badly provoked. I once had a Border bred from Champion Deerstone Destiny (which dates me somewhat); she would kill rats like lightning and even when badly nipped by an angry ferret she would run back, tail between her legs. She would, by way of contrast, thrash a fox to death underground. Borders are useful dyke dogs – they love water. Some people believe they have otter hound blood. If one's ratting patch is along a brook or river, the rat will readily take to water. Borders are ideal in such circumstances. I once hunted rat with Tony Bell and his dogs were the best I have ever seen hunting rats who have taken to water. I lost several pounds to Tony when we bet on whether or not his Borders would take a swimming, or diving, rat. They nearly always did.

Russells are a very mixed, unstandardised, bunch at the time of writing. Sadly the unscrupulous dealer will sell any short tailed, white bodied mongrel as a Russell. The would-be ratter would do well to buy from a reputable breeder. Most working Russells will make excellent ratting dogs, for many of the big Russell breeders and trainers look upon rats as starters, before moving their terriers on to more formidable quarry such as fox and badger. I am a Jack Russell addict; my finest ever dog on rat was a Russell. At the time when he was a puppy, to the time he was seven years old, I made a lot of money from competing against people who had "the best ratting terriers in Britain". He was a rough coated, ugly brute, no oil painting by any standard. He was treacherous with ferrets, and if I was not looking wicked with small babies whom he tried to drag from cots to shake to death, and many times I cursed him and threatened to shoot him, but when he died at the age of nineteen, he left a void in my life no other dog has filled.

How now to start your dog on rat? Firstly, and I repeat my advice on ferrets – go for a young animal that has not been ruined by other people. Buy a puppy and start by getting him used to the ferret – the ferret will usually correct overprecocity in a young puppy by a sharp nip, not the savage bite of a ferret out to kill, but merely a nip to say, "You are playing too roughly and I wish you to respect my dignity." Ferrets restrain themselves with a young puppy. Allow

Familiarity breeds a good working relationship.

your puppy to play with the ferret to get familiar with it. I have watched all kinds of hilarious games played between dogs and ferrets diving at each other out of cardboard boxes, and playing hide and seek. I actually encourage these games. They do not make either the dog or the ferret soft; they allow a common bond to form between them. Such a degree of familiarity will facilitate the dog knowing which is rat and which is ferret as they flash out of an earth. I once saw a dog so well broken to ferret that one day a rat bolted, slowly dragging the ferret which had anchored its teeth into the rat's rump. The dog quickly nipped the rat, killing it without shaking it, for a shake would probably have damaged the ferret. Such a familiarity is quite priceless in the sport which is so fast that a dog has to make instant decisions.

There is, however, one school of thought that believes a ratting terrier needs to learn how to kill rats before it is introduced to ferrets. There is, perhaps, some sound reasoning in this, as a terrier used to seeing a rodent like ferret leaping around and being told such a beast is *verboten* might be reluctant or slow to kill rats. While I respect this school of thought, for it has much logic to defend it, I do not agree with it. I have an odd feeling that many ferrets might bite the dust with a dog that is already an excellent rat killer and is, therefore, only too keen to slay anything that resembles a large rodent. I have seen many dogs trained by this method and they always seem to give the ferret a wistful look that should make shivers run up its musteline back.

We have discussed the bringing together of dog and ferret which, teamed up with man, we hope will make up a ratting triumvirate. Next let us discuss how we will enter your puppy to rat and once again shall I try to debunk yet another old wives tale which must be the oldest, and most illogical, rat dog training method devised. One simply takes out the puppy and dumps him in a barrel with a live adult rat. The logic of this method is that:

(1) the rat is frightened by the dog;
(2) the rat bites the dog;
(3) the dog is very angry indeed and bites the rat;
(4) the rat dies and the dog is started to rat.

It sounds all very logical, but sadly it is not as good a method as it sounds. True, it might work with a brash extrovert dog who would retaliate and kill the rodent. Maybe a typical Fell terrier/Lakeland would be only too ready to oblige the rat with a savage bite, but it is a fatal method to use on most dogs. It is enough to say that I have seen literally dozens of dogs ruined by this method of entering, labelled cowards, and rejected as useless by their owners. The fault is in the entering, not in the dog. Look at the method logically. Firstly, the dog has by now been prevented from chasing live-stock, usually by a sharp tap and a "No". It has experienced pain which it attacks, chases, or tries to harm any animal which is *verboten*. It is now placed in a barrel with twelve ounces of the most furious little creature God has made, and again it experiences pain, for bet your bottom dollar that rat will bite the dog. Might not the dog regard the rat as yet another animal not to be chased, hurt or harmed?

Well, how does one enter a dog to rat. The answer is *festina lente* – make haste slowly. One method is to take your dog at dusk to places where rats feed in number. Allow, and indeed encourage, him to chase them. He will miss great numbers before, one evening, he manages to connect and brings down his first rat. Praise him greatly for his prowess. Allow him one or two more kills – he will by now have improved out of recognition and will be ready to join the team of ferret, man, dog.

Another method is the "hot blood" method – a dog is taken out with a habitual rat killer. The puppy is tied up and allowed to see his teacher slaying rats with frenzy. He becomes frantic with excitement – mad for a chance to equal the other dog's feats. He is now slipped at a passing rat. He grabs it, bites it, and, being an amateur is savagely bitten in the bargain, but such is his state of excitement that he does not feel the pain and kills the rat. A few more kills and, *voilà* – a rat dog ready to join the team.

Take now your dog and ferret and if they are friendly enough, then allow them to drink from the same dish of milk before the hunt. Take them to a spot where there are rats a-plenty. If your dog is well entered then he will be more than a little excited by the scent of rats, and as he will have driven many to ground during his fruitless early chases, he will mark the holes that are inhabited. Don't, however, allow him to dig, bark or telegraph his presence to the rat below. The rat will know then that danger waits outside and will be reluctant to bolt. If he refuses to bolt he will "slug it out" with the ferret which is not what you want – a damaged ferret, a frustrated dog, and no rat at the end of the hunt. Allow the dog to merely sniff the hole. If he has an air of eager anticipation, restrain him. Do not over-encourage him, for some dogs will learn to mark or dig at any hole in order to please the owner – a little skill known as false marking and certainly not to be desired. Now take a good look at your location and watch for bolt holes. To give your terrier that extra chance (or equaliser, as we say in ratting circles) place a loose handful of grass into every bolt hole, and stuff it in very lightly – not firmly enough to prevent the rat from bolting. Push it in too tightly and neither ferret nor rat can remove the plug – result – again a frustrated hunt. Now, take your ferret from your box or bag, or what have you, and place her near the mouth of the earth. She will sniff the edges of the hole, tail held like a bottle brush. Some jills lash their tails from side to side when a hole is inhabited. (I once had a jill who was slightly afraid of rats and would not tackle them. She would, however, mark every inhabited hole by lashing her tail from side to side. The jill was the most accurate marking device I've ever encountered but you could never make her enter an inhabited hole. Funnily enough she died as a result of a bad rat bite one day when we were out after rabbit. There's an irony there, I believe.)

The ferret enters the rat hole and the terrier, quivering with excitement and anticipation, is held by you in a spot where the rat might just feasibly bolt. The excitement is intense, and the drumming you hear is your heart beating madly. A squeak, a thump, and your ferret has connected, a scurrying noise and the grass quivers as the rat goes to bolt. Out flashes rat, terrier flashes in, and the trio have made their first kill. Bravo! Eureka! and a few other self congratulations, but now comes the critical point. The ferret excited by the hunt emerges, her tail fluffed out. She has been actively engaged in a fight and she is flushed with excitement. The dog has made a kill. He is also excited with the pleasures of hunting. Do not touch your jill – many jills are very touchy after a battle with a rat, and bite one's hand savagely. My favourite jill – the tamest I've ever had, gave me a savage nip one day as I picked her up after a combat with a rat. Watch out, for now your ferret in its fury might nip the already excited dog, and you are in the middle of a load of trouble – with an angry dog shaking a very dead ferret as an encore to his rat killing exploit. Take the rat from the dog, allow your ferret to worry it and shake it. Don't allow her to drag it back down the hole. When she tires of worrying what she considers to be her kill, take her and put her back in the box and on to the next inhabited rat warren. Two or three kills like this and the team of dog, man and ferret is made.

I mentioned hand catching in my book on the Jack Russell, and have had thousands of letters asking how it is done. First piece of advice, if you are allowed a choice, don't do it – it is the deadliest game. If you are hell bent (and that is likely to be the correct expression) on trying, then, here comes the advice. Never, ever, listen to any countryman who tells you to grab your rat by the back of the neck – they are either telling you lies, or casting lustful glances at your future widow. This stupid tale has sent dozens of tyro rat catchers to their deaths, for fifty five percent of all rats carry deadly Wiel's disease (inoculate your dog always). Now for the concrete advice: place a wisp of grass in the bolt holes, as one of the wisps move, make ready with your foot when the rat emerges. Step lightly on the rat and hold him until his tail is clear of the earth. He will endeavour to bite your boot or shoe, but he will do little harm. I repeat, do not touch him until his tail leaves the hole. Pick him up before his tail leaves the hole and you may not only be bitten by the rat, but by the ferret following closely behind. The only safe way (I must be mad – no way is safe) to catch your rat is to tail him. He will try to turn, but unlike his mouse cousins, he cannot climb his own tail. Get him well away from your body, for in his fear he will urinate and his urine carries the deadly Wiel's disease far more than his bite. If the urine gets in a cut or graze, then you may well get infected. Hand catching is like playing Russian roulette with teeth. Lucas, in his immortal *Hunt and Working Terriers* mentions tailing the rat and flinging the rat up under your armpits. Don't waste your time. No adult rat can run up its tail, though if held close to the body its violent lunges and jerks allow it to grip any article of clothing or flesh near it. Its grip is like a bulldog. Once, when hand catching for a bet, I was holding a live, five week old baby, still in its grey coat, by the tail. The rat lunged and gripped a whip-like privet wand held by my friend. Fear and fury made its grip like a vice, and it held so tightly that it refused to let go, even when the privet wand was cracked and whirled around the head. They hold with a similar tenacity on human flesh, so beware! A local farmer was cleaning out the poultry muck under his battery pens. Something had jammed the roller, so he put his hand into the poultry manure to investigate. The cause of the stoppage was a large, pregnant doe trapped in the roller mechanism and manure. The rat bit his thumb and held on with beady eyes ablaze. It could not be choked off and had to be beheaded with a spade before it would release its grip. One more story to deter the would be hand catcher. At the 1976 Game Fair, Dave Ramsden, Secretary of The Fell and Moorland Working Terrier Club, told me a macabre story. Dave is well worth listening to, for he can tell a tale. He was hunting rat with a bank manager friend of his when the rat ran up into a hollow tree. The ferret followed, or tried to follow, for the ferret was unable to climb up inside the hollow tree. Dave's friend reached up to retrieve the ferret, but instead he grabbed the rat. The beast nipped his finger, but did not hold on. The thumb bled very little and was soon forgotten, but eight days later, Dave's friend was dead. Wiel's disease is a real killer. Since then Dave says that he has stayed clear of rats. Tom Evans, my first accurate naturalist friend, was by trade a rodent operative, which sounds more professional than rat catcher. He had a curious saying that had a great deal of wisdom in it: "Rat catching is easy when you know how, but the apprenticeship can be a bit of a bugger." Tom had many rat catcher colleagues that eventually died from the dreaded rat catcher's yellows, or Wiel's disease.

I suppose I have hunted just about every British wild animal, but I confess nothing is as exciting to me as a good rat hunt. Rats are numerous, unpopular, and regarded by most people as nasty, so places where one can hunt are usually easy to obtain. My diary, that I keep up to date daily, recalls some amazing adventures with rats. At one time I taught a particularly difficult class of boys who were reluctant to learn anything, and steadfastly refused to do any writing. At the weekends I sent up a prayer that it was Friday and got my ferrets, dogs and friends ready for the weekend's sport. I was in the process of clearing away the books from the last period of the day's riot, which was like Eisenstein's Battle On The Ice scene with chalk, when one of my most offensive lads piped up, "Whad der teachas do on weekends?", he added "Sir," so I knew he wasn't setting me up for a session's micky taking. I told them my weekend's activities truthfully. "Can we come, Sir?," was the cry of the whole class. As a refusal would result in a Monday morning hell for me, I cowardly said "Yes," for I knew most maladjusted boys don't turn up, but they all did. They learned to handle ferrets, hold terriers, whack rats, and had the day of their boring little lives. We took a bag of over a hundred in my first hour. My co-ratter lectured in English and said sarcastically, "Do you tell their parents it's educational?", and added, "The cure for his maladjustment, Madam, is to let him carry my ferret box for a few days." Curiously my friend was right. They talked about nothing else on Monday, wrote about rats, talked about rats, drew huge, badly proportioned rats on wall cards, and even sat through the entire Pied Piper poem without one fight taking place. My headmaster did not approve, however. He was a quaint, shrivelled up man, who was ready for premature burial at thirty and like most teachers of his age he was very boring. My kids were forced to write the customary "What I'd Like To Do When I Grow Up," for him. I glanced in and had the satisfaction of seeing they were giving him hell.

One day, however, while hunting the filthy maggot factory referred to by our staff as "Plummer's Estate", I had the most hellish experience. I had placed a good fiery black jill ferret in a rat hole, heard her connect with the rat, and a savage squealing fight had just taken place. One of my friends had suggested putting in another jill to help the first, but it would have been madness, for the second jill would have forced the first into the jaws of the rat, or prevented her from retreating if she had had enough. I refused and crouched near the earth, my jeans sweeping floor level, I was trying to find another hole to put in the second jill so that the rat was sandwiched between the two jills. There was another hole in the thick undergrowth, but I did not notice it as it was just beneath my jeans turn up. I crouched there, ferret in hand, listening to the battle boiling beneath my feet. The battle had ceased and the rat had decided to bolt. Bolt it did, straight up inside my trouser leg. It reached my knee before I came to my senses and grabbed it. "Tony", I croaked and numbled what had happened. "Easy," said Conners, and took up his ferret spade and dealt me a terrific blow on the leg. I screamed in agony. "Wrong leg, you bloody fool." He struck an even harder blow at the other leg and a pulped rat fell to the ground. So did I; paralysed with fear, I lay prostrate for nearly an hour while my "friend" sympathetically roared with laughter. On examining my leg, however, I found that, though smeared with rat blood, I was not bitten at all, nor were there any scratch marks. My brown rat had not intended to attack me, it had merely tried to evade my ferret and seek sanctuary in the darkness of my jeans.

Stories about rats leaping at one's throat, however, are ridiculous. When I hand caught many rats for a scientific research study at a university, I kept them in a barrel just under three feet high. Not one of them was able to jump out. No rat can leap three feet, let alone jump at one's throat. So, unless you are a dwarf, a very small child, or an African pigmy on an educational exchange visit, your throat is quite safe. Few rats really want to stay and make a fight of it, and even if cornered, desperately try to get away. I knew of only one rat that had the suicidal urge of a Kamikaze pilot. Once I ferreted a poultry house in Sutton Coldfield. I put in a white jill in a hole outside the shed and walked inside and put on the lights. We were not using dogs, as the birds were leghorn type hybrids which thrived in the battery cages, but went into bouts of feathery hysteria at the sight of a dog. Four pregnant doe rats bolted rapidly and we killed them with sticks. A big buck bolted and watched the scene from underneath the battery cages. My ferret followed him out, tail fluffed out and ready for action. I picked her up and boxed her, but as I did so the rat ran for the hole. He sniffed the hole and the strong scent of ferret caused him to turn. He then ran at me and attacked my shoes. I kicked him off and he squealed, but came back at me. I hit him, kicked him, but he was determined to have death or glory. At last I caught him a heavy blow and killed him. I wish

112

he could have escaped, he certainly deserved to. Did he decide to die to defend his does? Did the ferret scent deter him, or did he have some strange mental malady that prevented him from preserving his own life? I have caught countless thousand rats, but have only ever encountered one like him. Sadly I had to award his VC posthumously.

I have had few rat bites in spite of the fact that I enjoy ferreting rats. Only once did I experience a really nasty bite and then through my own nosey stupidity. I was ferreting the cavity between two badly constructed pig sties, for the man who owned it had an outbreak of some hideous pig disease that the vet said could be spread by rats. He would not restock his piggery until he was cleared of rats. I immediately volunteered. It was during the winter holidays, and I was bored. Also I needed the rats for ferret food and wanted to keep in with this very bad farmer who provided me with all his mortalities in his stock. So bad was his stockmanship that my ferrets lived on his dead stock. I decided to clear his sheds of rats, let him restock, and merely sit back and wait for the bags of dead piglets which I found on my way home from school. I put an elderly jill in between the walls and she found immediately – a squealing ensued. I looked over the wall to watch the carnage. The jill had released her rat, which ran up the wall and bit me a nasty one in the cheek. My face spouted with blood, and it was no consolation to look down and find that my jill had given up her rat hunt and was licking the blood which poured from my face. There's no loyalty in ferrets these days!

Some people can, and do, get away with some amazing feats with rats and ferrets. When I taught in Sheffield I hunted an old old tip near Mexborough. There was always a good supply of rats there and I never had a dead day. I trained my terriers on rats from this tip, as I was never troubled for trespass by the police, who often stopped to watch the sport (or was it me they watched?) I was having no luck today, however. My seven yearling terriers were tied in the van and were barking at the ferret as it bobbed out of each hole on its fruitless search. Suddenly I was aware I had an audience. My watcher had one of those ageless, lined faces and two large brown teeth. He looked rather like a walrus who had never heard of toothpaste. "Won't find any." I ignored him. "Just done 'em." I listened. "Want any for the terriers?" I nodded. "Two and a tanner," he said. "Two bob," said I, expecting a haggle.

"Done," he spat brown spittle on his palm and shook my hand. He was scruffily dressed in trousers, held up with a broad belt, and a filthy blood stained shirt. I looked around for his rat box or bag, but found none. "Turn puppy loose," he ordered, and I did so. He reached inside his shirt, drew out a squeaking rat. He shook it and threw it to the dog, who snapped it up. I paid Fred Cleaver, my new friend's name, fourteen shillings (70p), and he dropped each rat for the dogs. "Half a dollar for the last and a trick with it." I was too fascinated to haggle and paid him. He took my large white hob ferret from the liner box, and thrust it in his shirt. A squealing broke out and a grim fight began, finishing when my ferret began to dine and a spot of blood appeared on Cleaver's shirt. He fascinated me. "Any family?" I asked, convinced that all his kin had been carried off by the bubonic plague or salmonella or God knows what. "Wife left me," he said stonily. I couldn't help thinking I knew exactly why.

Fred became a nuisance in the end. At that time I had ideas far above my station, and pocket. There was a noted model living in the North, and I took her out. She was a dreadful plum in the mouth snob, and a frightful bore, but she was so good looking she impressed my friends. I borrowed a car from an opulent friend and borrowed money from my room mate. She had decided to see the country-side – a sort of rural slumming for her, but we were out of luck. At the first pub we found a slightly drunken Cleaver, with a shirt full of good things, and a huge hob ferret. I never saw my model again!

The reader will meet many such people who dice with death with rats and ferret. I have seen many idiots draw rats from a bag and bite them to death and yet suffer no ill effects from the trick – though I have always asked the landlord for "clean glasses" every round I bought for them. Other people have only to put their hands where a rat has urinated to become yellow corpses in a week or so. Different people have different constitutions, however. Last year I visited a friend of mine who told me Cleaver had caught a "flu bug" and died. Yet he was incredibly resistant to Wiel's disease.

It was on this same tip that I saw a sight that I had not seen before, nor have I seen since. We were offered many ferrets by the RSPCA, who found them wandering in the streets. Most police refused to touch them and they usually ended up with us. We usually thanked the RSPCA/police and gave the ferret away as a pet. They were usually quite useless for rat. They had also probably been lost through the evils of lying up or skulking and had to make a living in the town by either eating scraps or carrion, or perhaps even making a bid at young rats, but they had probably learned that the adult rat was too much for them and had gone back to carrion eating. Then, one day, I was offered a beautiful sandy jill ferret. She was a gem. She had been living wild for a month, yet was in incredibly good condition. Funnily enough the ferret had no inclination to bite or to spit, even after her month on the town. She was the most calm and phlegmatic ferret I have ever owned. I took her ratting the day she came to me and tried her on my tip. At first she bolted a litter of four week old greys and I allowed her to dine on one. On now to the next hole. Here we were not so lucky. My terrier marked. That there was a rat there was not in doubt. I put in the jill – a slight scuffle and she came out tail first, and looked into the hole. I picked her up – she was unmarked. I put her in again and again she backed out tail fluffed like a bottle brush and spitting like a fury. A large doe rat followed her out and attacked her in the open, slashing and nipping at my squealing ferret. She seemed quite blind to the fact that we were there. My terrier was also just a little baffled – he couldn't make up his mind as to whether he should sort out the rat from the ferret, for he had been smacked for giving the ferret a funny look. The doe now flashed back into the hole. Curious about the amazing sight I had just witnessed, I put my ferreting spade in and gently shifted some earth. A few inches in the doe crouched in the nest with the newly born litter. I pushed back the earth, and left her. To kill such a valiant creature would have been a sin. Hunting is only a brutaliser of people when men fail to recognise and reward the courage of their prey. I believe half the cave drawings so vividly done were drawings of the game ones who got away. It was primitive man's way of showing his respect. I too showed my respect. I left my valiant doe and her young and tried another hole, but by now my sandy jill had decided rats were too much for her, and she refused to enter the other nest.

Matthews, and several other writers, make mention of the fact that in spite of the ferret's bloodthirsty nature, many jills show a marked interest in adopting the young of other species, even the young of animals that ferrets find mortal enemies. Matthews is but one of the people who make mention of the ratting ferret who was given a litter of baby rats to eat alive. She ate three, but the subsequent squeaking of the fourth aroused some strange maternal instinct within her, for she took the remaining young rat to her nest and reared it with her own two day old litter. It lived happily with its strange foster brothers though the fact that the rat matured at a far greater speed than the kit ferrets caused the jill some concern, for the rat ran about the hutch at three weeks old and the mother ferret raced out, grabbed her, and brought her back to the nest. The jill slew other rats with great fury, but tended her foster child with all the love and affection she gave to her own litter. I believe this story, as I saw two examples of similar occurrences that confirmed this peculiar fostering instinct. A few weeks ago my kennel lad left the cage front of the ferret pen slightly open. The jill escaped and we found the squashed body of the jill on the road outside my cottage. I was faced with a problem. I had a litter of young ferrets, three weeks old, and no mother. I once reared a stoat from this age, or tried to rear him, for he didn't respond to the lactol substitute and died. I did not, therefore, welcome the chance of rearing nine young ferrets to maturity. I half filled a bucket of water to finish the orphans, when an idea came to me, I had another jill with young three days older. I placed the orphans in the dung corner and waited. The jill stuck her head out of the box and came to investigate, but to my horror, tail like a bottle brush. She sniffed the orphans and returned to her nest. The day was chilly, and the dung corner cold. The young began to squeal at the chill. Again the jill's head appeared, her maternal instinct playing hell with her commonsense. With a rather erratic manner she took the orphans to her box and reared the twelve. I once tried to foster a stoat with some ferrets. They mingled well and I was convinced I would rear and probably produce a hybrid stoat/ferret (man alive, what a hunter's dream). The experiment would have been a success as well, but the hot summer killed the whole litter, stoat as well – though curiously my stoat was the last to go.

My next reason for believing Matthews' strange tale is totally dissimilar to the last. Jeff Elwood and I hunted rat along a brook which ran near my cottage. The doe rat had decided to bolt, but could not as Jeff's jill – a real hell cat – held her by the rump. We killed the doe, let the jill worry the body and she went back into the hole. We all expected the buck to bolt, but in a moment the jill appeared carrying a live, gentle, young rat. It was quiet and gentle because the jill carried it as she did her own young. "Are you taking the dead doe back to feed the young ferrets, Jeff?" "I lost them all," said Jeff. Something clicked. Did the rat baby resemble her own and did the tiny squeaking resemble the litter of her own that finished its life squealing quietly as they died of *E. coli*. I had no doubt that the jill was ready to adopt the young rat. I suggested Jeff took both home and tried to rear the baby rat. Rats are interesting, but to Jeff the thought of infecting his two children with Wiels disease exceeded his interest in the psychology of convincing a jill it could rear a baby rat. Jeff knocked the baby on the head. I could not help thinking the jill was slightly distressed by Jeff's actions. I was certain that Jeff's jill would rear this rat. One needs a Ministry of Agriculture permit to rear the rats, but they are usually granted as the Ministry would either think that the applicant was a scientist or quite simply a lunatic. I also doubt if any Ministry official would have the nerve to tell you to destroy a rat reared in captivity by a ferret anyway. Drabble did rear a wild rat, as did Frances Pitt, but although they are reported to make excellent, lively, pets, they are not for me. Even when tamed, brown rats are alive with Wiels disease.

So, reader, I bring you to the end of the chapter on the hunting of the rat with the ferret. If you turn up at a farm with good ferrets, well trained dogs, and a team of friends who are not so stupid as to chase after rats and allow the ferret to wreak havoc on the poultry, then you will not be welcomed back. Making a good reputation is hard, destroying it is remarkably easy. Furthermore, although few men can conceal their hatred of rats, never allow your friends to commit acts of wanton cruelty against them. Kill them, but for heaven's sake kill them quickly. Don't bait or torture them to death. It brutalises the men and gives the anti-bloodsport society all the ammunition it needs. Don't give this society the ammunition it needs. If one kills, kill quickly and painlessly.

9 Sundry Ferret Uses

Rabbits are amazing creatures, for not only are they the food of foxes etc., the actual fox earth usually starts out with a pregnant vixen enlarging the warren to get at some unhappy rabbit, but leaves the terrified tenant in one of the minor original tunnels, and then has her cubs in the now enlarged warren. It has been estimated that over eighty per cent of fox earths started out as rabbit warrens. Curiously, in spite of the fact the fox is inhabiting the actual central cavity of the warren, the rabbits continue to breed in the minor galleries, sharing a somewhat uneasy tenancy. We once had a bitch go to ground in a deep fox earth in Bridgnorth. So deep was she in that we spent twenty-nine hours digging her out. We sank a huge trench in the ground and on the way down to the vixen encountered several nests of rabbits. All manner of beasts live, I could hardly say in harmony, in a rabbit earth.

Ernie Phillips once bolted a cat from a rabbit earth with a large hob ferret. The local farmer said that the cat had reared several litters of kittens in these earths. Rabbits also lived in the galleries of this warren and Ernie netted three rabbits from the same warren. Question, how does one get one very tangled cat out of a purse net, and still remain in one piece. Ernie assures me he let the cat out alive, but a cat tangled in a net takes some releasing. I should have been fascinated to watch. Even rabbits get very tangled up in these nets sometimes. I had a very bad kicking from a large buck rabbit that I had tried to take alive to restock an ash tip we were hunting in Birmingham. We caught the buck, a three and a half pounder – big for a wild rabbit, in my nets in Hilton, Derby. He hit the nets as normal, but most rabbits lie quite still when the purse net tightens. This one was different, however, for he began to gyrate like a dervish. Never was a net more tangled. I unravelled the net and tried to take him out, but as I wanted him alive, I did not want him hurt. The rabbit used his hind legs to good advantage and raked my arms and face dreadfully before I managed to free him. How Ernie

118

finally released his cat alive is still a mystery. Once I unsnared a cat for some police officers who thought that for once my knowledge of biology would come in useful in freeing the cat. I asked if their knowledge of first aid would come in useful for treating my wounds, for the cat fought like mad. If one hits your nets and you want to extricate it alive, then the best of luck to you.

Rats, of course, regularly inhabit rabbit warrens and particularly if the warrens are near farm buildings. This fact probably gave rise to the country legend, popular around this district, that rats will quite freely hybridise with rabbits. This is, of course, completely untrue. One warren I hunted when I was making a meagre living as a rabbit catcher, was so infested with rats that I used to station an obedient terrier near the earth to nail the rats as they skipped through the nets. Most people in the nearby village believed in this rat-cum-rabbit hybrid idea, for many local rabbits had short ears, and I found it very difficult to sell the poached rabbits to the locals, most of whom looked on rabbits with disgust. I had one very bad time trying to sell rabbits poached from the land of a local skinflint who had the nerve to let his ill kept land as a shoot – and at a very high price. His land bordered the railway line – always a good bet for rabbits. One day we ferreted this line. With great luck we took fifty-two, an enormous number for the post myxomatosis days. Now we were faced with a problem and indeed it was a problem. To get rid of two or three rabbits is easy – a visit to a pub, or better still, our local lorry drivers cafe would be enough to do this, but fifty!! If we tried to sell to a game shop the police and shop keeper would probably ask where we had obtained such a number. It was Saturday, so they'd be pretty smelly by the time the Friday market came. It was indeed a problem. Mark, ever the brains of our outfit, came to the rescue with one of his usual brainwaves. He always turned up at our poaching outings immaculately dressed. This helped him in two ways. Firstly, if we were caught, he could and would deny any knowledge of the two filthy ruffians with him. Secondly, he knew he was well dressed and immaculate, and if a jill decided to lie up we would not ask him to dig and spoil his clothes. Mark, dressed smartly, put the rabbits in the boot of his Fiat and calmly drove up to the farm. I could not help thinking that he looked like a typical TV type bishop, not an absolutely unscrupulous poacher. He calmly knocked on the door of the farm we had just poached. Now Scrooge was famed for his meanness and in spite of the fact he let the shoot, he would only allow the shoot to keep a brace of rabbits and took the rest for himself, storing them in his deep freeze until he had enough for the game shops job lot. "We seem to have a surfeit of rabbits from our shoot down the road." Mark pointed aimlessly. We had no shoot. "Would you care to give us, say, a nominal price for the lot, as it's such a damned drag selling them in the town." Scrooge's eyes gleamed and he offered Mark a sum far too low, but seeing Mark's impassive face he increased his figure slightly. "Sounds reasonable," said Mark, parting with the rabbits and taking the old miser's money. They were from his farm anyway, and meanness such as his should not go unrewarded. We left, feeling a little like Edgar Wallace's "Five Just Men", not the poaching rogues we were.

If one is quiet, and one should always be when ferreting, then just now and again a fox will sneak out of the earth and hit your nets – though he will usually manage to pull out the peg and take the net with him, throwing off the nets a few fields later. Foxes take nets out like lightning and one has to be very quick to nab them. Once I was lucky. My ferret, a large hob, too big for my liking, but quiet and quick, entered the earth rapidly. There was a scurrying noise, not like the bumping of a rabbit making up its mind to bolt. The net tightened, and the peg began to pull out. I grabbed it and held on, feeling a little like St Peter must have felt when he cast the net on the right side of the ship. The net held a twenty-two pound vixen. I caught this vixen and killed her quietly and quickly. We were hunting a railway embankment and again we had no permission (I won't mention where). Merely trespassing on railway property is a prosecutable offence and trespass in pursuit of God knows what is certainly one for the magistrates courts in the morning. I was reluctant to hunt these places as I knew that if I had a conviction for poaching in these places I had no chance of getting back into teaching – though at that time rabbit catching was far more lucrative, but once again, I reckoned without the mental agility of Mark and Ernie. Mark and Ernie bought dungarees and flat shovels were borrowed from the local tar laying firm. While I was ferreting madly in the undergrowth with net in hand and fear in heart, Mark and Ernie gently poked at the white limestone of the track. They waved to passing train drivers who waved back and smiled. We took a fantastic haul, for Ernie's brother had a friend in the game trade who didn't ask too many questions. Still, after a week, I was

120

getting distinguished grey hairs on the side of my head. Ernie did not help by joking, "If you are caught they will obviously consider you a poacher, but they will simply write us off as two lunatics." We were never caught. One day two railway police came slowly and ominously towards Ernie and Mark. This was the end. I was ferreting in deep cover, and my heart missed a beat. This was it. Photograph with a number across my chest – Plummer, D. B. Goodbye teaching post, goodbye lectureship – the end. Not so, for I reckoned without Mark's superb mental agility, so out of place in a body this size. He almost ordered the police to him. "Since they've used limestone instead of slag for packing," he said, "there has been a decided decline in railway stability." He invited the police to crack a piece of limestone and then a piece of slag, with what they must have considered to be geological hammers. Actually they had just been used for hammering in the pegs for purse nets. "False economy – we'll be like the bloody Continent," he raged. ("Patriotism," says Dr Johnson, "is the last refuge of the scoundrel.") Mark then went into an involved lecture on the price of slag as opposed to limestone and gave such a boring talk that the two railway police were desperate to get away. In the meanwhile I crouched in the bushes with two dead rabbits and the beginnings of a nervous ulcer.

Lucas, in his classic terrier book, *Hunt and Working Terriers,* mentions that many hunts did not use terriers to bolt fresh foxes, but relied on huge hob ferrets who trundled down the hole and bolted the confused fox. However, if a fox is driven to ground by hounds, it is madness to put in a ferret for it is sure to be chopped in two. Bill Brockley, the Midland terrier man, tells a tale of his youth when he palled around with a gamekeeper in Bilston, Leicestershire. His keeper friend had put a jill into a drain that normally held rabbits. It was a big drain and very wide, and it would have been wiser to have blocked the end and used a terrier. There was a scuffle, but the jill did not come out. "She has killed in," said Bill, and got the line on the big hob ferret. The hob trundled up the pipe and another scuffle and the line went slack. Bill pulled the line and the hob, disembowelled and quite dead, was pulled out. "The —," said the keeper. "A bloody fox." He reached for his twelve bore and fired two barrels straight up the drain. The noise was enough to kill the vixen, let alone the number five shot. Bill put in his ugly old veteran, Rusty, who drew out a dreadfully mangled fox.

Stoats, like rats, often bolt from warrens when one is ferreting –

skipping through the nets with contemptuous ease. Stoats are fascinating and curious animals. As I explained in Chapter One, the stoat's very name means valiant and bold, but funnily enough, they bolt every time to a ferret. If one shoots at a bolted rabbit and it goes back to ground, then there is little chance of it bolting again. He will lie up in the blind hole and await his death rather than face gun or dog again. A rat, so pushed, will nearly always refuse to bolt twice and subsequently try to slug it out with the ferret. Stoats, on the other hand, seem to have a mortal fear of the ferret and will bolt to it time and time again. This is an enigma – for no matter how one looks at it, the stoat which is the size of a jill ferret and has twice the biting speed, must be more than a match for a ferret. God knows they have the cutlery to deal out the damage to a ferret, yet they always give ground when a jill is put in against one. Why they bolt, heaven only knows. Maybe they have a great fear of the ferret, but I have a sneaking respect for the stoat and I should like to feel that he was prepared to take his chances against the foes above ground. Unscientific and over-romantic, but...?

10 Disease

Any book on gamekeeping and ferreting will inform the readers that only three maladies trouble the ferret, sweats, mange and foot rot. Sadly, the ferret is very prone to an amazing variety of maladies and sadder still, little is known about their causes. A lot is known about their effects – which is quite simply death. Furthermore, you will find little satisfaction in going to the vet with your sick ferret, for there is very little known about musteline infections. All your vet will do is to administer a shot of antibiotic – and pray. Frankly little research has been done on ferret infection. Certainly the books on ferret stockmanship are few and far between, and the remedies suggested for disorders are like something out of medieval grimoires. Any book written by a warrener or ex-gamekeeper, will instantly label any lethal infection as the "sweats" an all encompassing term for anything that will kill ferrets, stoats and weasels.

Mink, however, the highly commercial cousin of the ferret, has had a great deal of money ploughed into the research projects on musteline diseases and are so similar to ferrets that they are useful creatures to read about. The humble ferret has had little research money ploughed into its study. In desperation I wrote to one of the last of the German fitch farmers still alive. He was polite in a Prussian way, but stated that fitch farmers in Germany accepted the deaths of their stock stoically as there was then no knowledge of antibiotics and little satisfactory research had been done on infections such as canine distemper – the real sweats in ferrets. Now new fitch farmers have started up in the south of England – perhaps now that the fur is commercial new research will be done into ferret diseases. Until then the ferret breeder will have to make do with the limited amount of research I have uncovered about the diseases of the ferret. Reader, I bid you read on, for though this chapter may not have the interest of the previous ones, it is the most important, for not only is it some of the only scientific research written on the ferret, it is indeed the record of my own errors and mistakes and should be written in tears, not printer's ink.

Let us now begin with the simple diseases which are fairly easily treated.

Mange

Ferret mange is caused by a tiny mite called the sarcoptic mite. It can also be caused by a sarcoptic mite of a slightly different type found on foxes. Whichever mite causes it, it looks very nasty. The mite causes intense irritation – I know it is called scabies in humans and when I contracted it, the itching nearly drove me mad. Ferrets feel the same way about it and scratch madly. At one time I killed foxes for bounty, or tally money, as local farmers called it. I "boned out" the tail, gave the brush to the farmer, and fed the carcase to the ferrets. They nearly all contracted mange, for they were fed foxes regularly. After a while I got wise to why and skinned my foxes and stopped feeding unskinned carcases. My mange problem came to a sudden halt. Rats, particularly old rats, often carry sarcoptic mange, and I avoid feeding suspect rats to my ferrets. I used to use a lot of these suspect rats to feed my goshawk who did not contract mange.

Early ferret books state that mange is caused purely by filthy cages. True, the disease is helped along by filthy bedding, but it is not the cause of the trouble. Rat hunting ferrets and ferrets which hunt the warrens of rabbits that have harboured foxes pick up mange sometimes. They scratch madly, the fur becomes thin and the skin very red.

Well, now the reader will know all about how to recognise mange. Next, how to treat it. Firstly, mange mites can live in the woodwork. If your shed is old, burn it. If it is reasonably good, then follow the instructions to the letter. Remove your ferret, and place him in a disposable box. His carrying box will do for a while. Clean out his cage with a scraper and go over the woodwork with the flame of a blowlamp. When the shed is cool, creosote it. The dry wood will absorb the creosote readily. Add a little sulphur to the creosote and the shed will become mange resistant. Leave the ferret pen for about a day before re-introducing the ferret.

Next, however, to treat the ferret. Several good mange dips are available. Old time keepers used mixtures of vaseline, or thick motor oil, and boiled the liquids up adding sulphur until it forms a thick yellow paste. It is nasty, unpleasant, but quite effective. It was not only used on ferrets. Mother Allens Mixture, a quack medicine sold

124

around fairs as a specific for lice and scabies, used this mixture as a cure all. It leaves the ferret looking greasy, sad and dejected. Avoid like the plague the creosote and sulphur mixtures advised by early rat catchers. The irritation causes scratching and the creosote in an open wound is agonising. Creosote rarely cures ferrets. It literally kills them. Never use creosote on any living animal.

I used to use liver of sulphur as a dip, though it gives off fumes that smell of rotten eggs. It is highly effective, deadly to mange mites, and other skin parasites including fleas, lice and tics. It also imparts a curious sheen to a ferret's coat when the fur grows back. Furthermore, although it stings slightly, the side effects are not nearly as deadly as the newer, more complex, mangicides. Liver of sulphur, or to give it its proper name, potassium sulphide, is difficult to obtain, but if one can find a chemist that stocks it, buy it up. Keep it in a tightly sealed jar, however, as the substance loses its value if left open to the air. Two or three dips will usually do the trick and the hair will grow back in six weeks.

Yet another useful medicine is the emulsion known as benzyl benzoate. This is a human scabies remedy and is harmless if kept off the vagina of the female or scrotum of the hob. It stings. Cover only half the ferret each day, for to seal off all the pores in the body would result in the benzoate being absorbed and the ferret dying. Repeat these dressings for a week and no trace of mange will usually be found. Again, don't expect instant hair growth. That takes three to six weeks to regrow.

The most effective remedy is, alas, quite dangerous for some ferrets react to it with thrashing fits, others suffer no ill effects. The chemical of which I speak is gamma benzene hexachloride. Don't be frightened by the name, it is sold under various names, BHC, Lorexane, Gammexane. It is also the active chemical in Coopers Mange Dip for dogs, and in most sheep dips. If used at slightly weaker doses than recommended for dogs, sheep and pigs, then the chemical is most efficient. Used in a stronger dose it is an even better mange deterrent – for your ferret will die. If you have the courage to go to the chemist and ask for Lorexane Louse Lotion, you are on a winner. This is simply BHC dissolved in an alcohol or ether base. It works wonderfully on a ferret and is neither greasy nor nasty smelling. You will get some odd looks from the girl at the chemists, however. Prioderm, as used on children's heads, is another priceless mange remedy – if one can obtain it. It works in about four days and there is absolutely no danger of harming the ferret. It also does not irritate and has a pleasant smell. It is quite difficult to obtain however.

Tetmosol is the latest rage in dog mange control and as dog mange is usually the same sarcoptic mite that attacks ferrets – then you can rely on this chemical. A word in your ear first. If used in not too strong a dosage it is priceless. If one exceeds the dosage by merely a fraction then you will find that your ferret is likely to be dead. It will, however, if used in moderation cure mange in ferrets, or in dogs for that matter, in a matter of ten days. But reader beware, do not experiment with this deadly chemical.

Foot Rot

This highly unpleasant condition was once the scourge of ferret keepers, but now, owing to improved general hygiene the condition is considerably more rare. It is caused by a fungus, the spores of which will live for many years in the crevices of the woodwork of the ferret cage. It is, therefore, difficult to cure and symptomatic of neglect. If a ferret is kept in a wet, slimy, cage then the ferreter is just asking for an invasion of this unpleasant infection. If, on the other hand, the ferret is kept on clean deal shavings, cleaned out daily, or perhaps on a wire floor, then I doubt if he will find his ferret experiences the full hell of foot rot. One word of advice. Foot rot literally does eat the feet away, so it is useless putting an infected ferret on the floor of wire and expecting a cure. The poor beast is in a fair amount of pain, and subsequently the wire floor really does damage the already injured foot tissue. Clear the infection first. This is easier said than done however. Many ferret keepers advise a sharp knock on the head as the cure – it certainly clears up the infection – but still leaves the hutch full of spores. Better to try and clear the infection and clean the hutch. The disease is cured only with difficulty and takes considerable time, but if you are prepared to persist it can be cured. Firstly get a load of deal shavings for bedding and decide to clean it every day. Paint the floors of the hutch with a weak solution of copper sulphate and allow it to dry. Another coat of creosote on top should seal off any traces of copper sulphate and preserve the wood. All fungal spores should now be dead. Next treat the ferret. Old gamekeepers used the oil and sulphur mix which is not really effective. Iodine, if the flesh is not too raw, gentian violet, Mycota – one of the best creams available and easily obtained as it is used for athletes foot, are all useful remedies. Once you have cleared the ferret do keep the floor clean and prevent any chance of the return of the dreaded foot rot. One of the only untreatable cases of foot rot I have ever encountered was with a ferret kept by a boy in Reading. He asked me to look at it as it was lame. The fungus had eaten away the pads and pieces of naked bone showed through the tattered flesh. Treat foot rot as soon as you see it.

Sweats

Now reader, I bid you beware – you will finish these few paragraphs in despair. Sweats is the old time, all time killer of ferrets. Quite simply it is distemper – yes, the same disease that is found in dogs. Some strains of distemper merely make a dog ill for four or five days and then they recover and get back to normal. All strains of canine distemper are fatal to a ferret. Ancient books recommend sweet tincture of silver (whatever that is) others recommend rhubarb root – a specific for most ailments in small animals a few centuries ago and a supposedly useful stimulant to a running dog who is off its food. As a cure for distemper or sweats – alas, there is nothing you can do once the disease has set in. No antibiotic has any effect on the sweats virus, so forget wasting your money at the vets. One can, however, get one's ferret inoculated against distemper. One dose of dog distemper vaccine is enough for four ferrets, so, for say 50p a time one can inoculate all one's ferrets. I inoculate mine against this ferret distemper. If one has a friend at a mink farm he can usually obtain the vaccine very much cheaper. The best time to inoculate ferrets is about twelve weeks – after they have lost their maternal immunity.

Feline Infectious Enteritis

If one notices that most of the cats are dying in your district – beware! The disease is feline infectious enteritis. It kills roughly ninety per cent of the cats in infects and also makes considerable inroads into the ferret population. Alas, again, this is a deadly virus, so again forget your visit to the vets. His antibiotics will do no good. One can inject a vaccine to prevent this disease, but it is expensive. One dose of cat vaccine will usually be enough to serve four ferrets.

Post-Nest Deaths

Now we hit the really big problem with ferrets and the answer to it is still very much in doubt. When young ferrets leave the nest

127

to feed there is usually a very high mortality in some litters. Many breeders never experience this, while others lose whole litters.

Jeff Elwood and Moses Smith, both expert ferret keepers have failed to rear a litter in 1976 as a result of this malady. Before I attempt to try to solve the problem – again called sweats by the old ferret books, let us look at the symptoms.

(a) litters born early in the year rarely die from what I shall now call post-nest deaths.

(b) the deaths occur when the young are usually twenty-eight to thirty-six days old.

(c) Whole litters die off sometimes and the dung corner is full of very liquid faeces.

(d) I have found litters of stoats also dying of these symptoms, so the disease is not confined to ferrets.

(e) the deaths occur very quickly – the young will be dead in a matter of hours.

(f) curiously losses among slop fed ferrets are usually lower than those found in properly reared litters.

(g) the jill is rarely even ill, though she is often very agitated by the deaths of her young.

I lost four litters of flesh fed ferrets during 1973. They were fed chicken entrails and paunch or tripe. All were kept clean and the food was always fresh. Autopsied ferrets revealed a very high build up of *E. coli* (a type of gut bug) but all creatures have these micro organisms living inside them and it is only when the *E. coli* population becomes large that deaths occur.

I was quite convinced my entire crop was for burying, though no adult ferret died, but by a stroke of luck my deep freeze broke down and chicken offal goes very rank quickly. We boiled the offal and fed it. The whole crop were dying anyway, so I had little to lose. Strangely all deaths stopped from that day on. Why?!! I believe my feeding of raw guts added either a new variety of *E. coli*, or added to the already high proportion of coli in the ferret entrails. By boiling the offal I killed the new coli. Many people believe that this coli bug is responsible for reducing predators so that they do not become too numerous. It certainly doesn't help when one is trying to rear ferrets. We cook the entrails and meat from the time the ferret young are ten days old and then feed raw bloody carcases of rats, etc., from the time when the ferret kits are nearly five months old. I have not had a dose of post-nest deaths since.